The Mysticism of Ordinary and Extraordinary Experience

The Mysticism of Ordinary and Extraordinary Experience

Harry L. Serio

Foreword by Dale E. Graff

RESOURCE *Publications* • Eugene, Oregon

THE MYSTICISM OF ORDINARY AND EXTRAORDINARY EXPERIENCE

Copyright © 2021 Harry L. Serio. All rights reserved. Except for brief quotations in critical publications or reviews, no part of this book may be reproduced in any manner without prior written permission from the publisher. Write: Permissions, Wipf and Stock Publishers, 199 W. 8th Ave., Suite 3, Eugene, OR 97401.

Resource Publications
An Imprint of Wipf and Stock Publishers
199 W. 8th Ave., Suite 3
Eugene, OR 97401

www.wipfandstock.com

PAPERBACK ISBN: 978-1-7252-9101-0
HARDCOVER ISBN: 978-1-7252-9100-3
EBOOK ISBN: 978-1-7252-9102-7

04/08/21

Scripture quotations are from New Revised Standard Version Bible, copyright © 1989 National Council of the Churches of Christ in the United States of America. Used by permission. All rights reserved worldwide.

LOST IN THE STARS. Words by MAXWELL ANDERSON. Music by KURT WEILL. © 1946 (Renewed) CHAPPELL & CO., INC. and TRO–HAMPSHIRE HOUSE PUBLISHING CORP. All Rights Reserved. Used by Permission of ALFRED MUSIC.

LOST IN THE STARS. From the Musical Production "Lost In The Stars". Words by Maxwell Anderson, Music by Kurt Weill. TRO- © Copyright 1944 (Renewed) 1946 (Renewed) Hampshire House Publishing Corp., New York, NY and Chappell & Co., Los Angeles, CA. International Copyright Secured. Made in U.S.A. All Rights Reserved Including Public Performance For Profit. Used by Permission.

Contents

Foreword by Dale E. Graff | vii
Preface | ix

The Nature of Mystical Experiences | 1
The Conscious Universe | 13
Things That Go Bump in the Night | 19
Episodes in the Life of a House | 25
Spirits among Us | 34
Seance in the Sanctuary | 37
Unexpected Visitors | 44
Deathbed Visions and Near-Death Experiences | 46
The Exorcist | 53
Born Again . . . and Again . . . and Again | 58
Death of a Young Girl in Springtime | 68
Liminality at the Time of Death | 72
   Transitions of the Soul as a Rite of Passage
"I Told You So!" | 83
The Future Is Not What It Used to Be | 85
Time and Again | 90
Sacred Places | 92
From Deep to Deep | 97
American Poustinia | 103
Dasein | 108
Breath of God | 112
Room of Contemplation | 115

In the Breaking of Bread | 118
One without a Name | 121
Objects | 124
Emmanuel | 128
Mysticism of Jazz | 131
Sexual Mysticism | 148
Folk Spirituality of the Pennsylvania Dutch | 152
Parataxic Totemization | 157
The Defenestration of the Soul | 160
Avatar | 163
   Exploring Things Visible and Invisible
Walkers between Worlds | 166
   The Celtic Mystic Tradition in a Postmodern Age
Entering the Cloud of Unknowing | 175
Make Light of Yourself | 178
To See Ourselves | 180
Lost in the Stars | 182
Killing the Buddha | 185

Bibliography | 189

Foreword

WHEN READING DR. HARRY Serio's book, *The Mysticism of Ordinary and Extraordinary Experience*, you become a time traveler, an explorer through space and time. In these excellent pages, you are privileged to experience a wide range of cultural and religious history including those regions described by the poets, writers, philosophers, mystics, and theologians, along with others who venture between the boundaries of the seen and unseen.

Dr. Serio's thorough description of the roots of religion spanning many diverse cultures and the impact these had on the Christian-Judaic tradition places this heritage into a global historic context. This is valuable for bringing together, for re-uniting, all of us regardless of specific creed, as we search for understanding our connections with the great mysteries of life and for discovering our essence at deep levels of being.

Dr. Serio explains how religion and science are searching into the same mystery, and acknowledges how ancient understanding of energy and vibrations are compatible with modern concepts in quantum physics with its interconnectedness of all things. He reviews current findings in physics and brainwave research that illustrates his scope of interest and how science and religion can be understood as different ways of describing the mysteries of creation.

He includes many of his personal experiences that help the reader understand his struggles with reconciling them within the traditional understandings. Some of these experiences clearly illustrate the potential that we all have for accessing these mysteries and benefitting from them in practical situations, such as perceiving information from the future in premonitions. He considers chance and its meaningful counterpart, synchronicity, and that intentionality of a universal design is subtlety evident in the events of

Foreword

our lives and the evolving universe. Throughout his book, Dr. Serio interjects humor to illustrate the importance of humility for our understandings and for our relationships. His detailed accounts of Celtic historic connections provide a context for those of us who resonate with bridge building, whether it be between various religions perspectives or between science and religion. This follows from a consistent theme throughout his book; the unity of all things and the realization that a universal consciousness is everywhere. We are part of the Whole. He weaves this perspective with a theological framework and a naturalistic worldview. Dr. Serio's thoughtful discussion of time and river metaphors, that often appear in literary works, and the connection between heroic journeys from the Odyssey to classic myths for modern times illustrates the immense scope of his writings. Dr. Serio's deep connection with jazz, and his role in bringing jazz to the Reading, PA area through a two-week annual event attests to the power of music and that spirituality can be found in the spaces where music from the soul resides. The natural rhythm of such music resonates with our deep psyche and is a unifying experience, bringing together, re-uniting us with our ancient roots and the creative principles of the universe.

Now the COVID-19 virus has come into our contemporary lives. Dr. Serio's discussion of being present considers the impact of social distancing on our lives. He wonders if holographic projection will become a new communication technique and if too much reliance on electronic means will bring us closer together, or lead to further separation.

There are many topics in this book that will inspire us to dig deeper into our own history and to ponder our destiny. Dr. Serio's book brings us into a deeper understanding of ourselves and others and that the ordinary and extraordinary are an integral aspect of all us. He inspires us to explore and discover this for ourselves.

Dale E. Graff
Aerospace Engineer (ret.)
Founder and Former Director
United States Government's
PROJECT STARGATE

Preface

ALMOST EVERYONE HAS HAD mystical experiences but may not have recognized them as such. These include times of deep peace, total relaxation free from any cares or worries, an awareness of another reality or state of being that encompasses one's total essence. There may also be extraordinary experiences, encounters with the paranormal, including beings not physically present. Some of these experiences may be revelatory in which information or insight is received without any reason or deliberate cognition. There may also be a profound sense of being loved, of being part of a universal consciousness which many mystics often regard as God. Each person has this potential and therefore anyone may be regarded as a mystic when he or she is open to a greater awareness of the presence of God.

There are persons who are regarded as mystics in all of the world's religions, and there are groups within many spiritual expressions that deliberately seek to cultivate the mystical experience. Mysticism has been studied from various perspectives including historical, theological, psychological, and scientific.

As a pastor in the United Church of Christ I have tried to be sensitive to the reporting of unusual experiences by members of the congregations I have served and by those who were referred to me by my ministerial colleagues. I have encouraged my fellow clergy to listen to the stories of their parishioners with openness and to be prepared to discuss how these experiences may have impacted their lives and their understanding of the nature of reality and their relationship with God.

I have included in these pages accounts of my own experiences, times when I became more aware of the presence of God in my life and of my own relationship with a universal consciousness. My personal encounters with the paranormal have led me to further research. I became president of the

Preface

Academy for Spiritual and Consciousness Studies. Inc. and have presented papers at their annual conferences. Some of the chapters in this book were offered at these conferences.

The first chapter, "The Nature of Mystical Experiences," is adapted from my doctoral dissertation at Lancaster Theological Seminary: "Mysticism and Ministry: A Descriptive Inquiry Into the Varieties of Mystical Experiences Among United Church of Christ People in Berks County, Pennsylvania (1992).

I have attempted to cite all the references that I have used. However, I apologize if I have missed any.

I am grateful to those who have shared their experiences with me, whether normal or paranormal, and who have offered helpful suggestions, particularly my wife Mary Ann Serio, and children, Tasha, Stuart, and Matthew. I also appreciate the encouragement of friends and colleagues who read and endorsed the manuscript: Dr. Lee S. Barrett, professor of New Testament at Lancaster Theological Seminary; astrophysicist Dale Graff, with whom I have co-presented several lectures on related subjects; and Dr. Mark D. Rader, physician and long-time friend.

The Nature of Mystical Experiences

THE "DIRECT APPREHENSION" OF the divine would be a simple definition of "mysticism," but mysticism is anything but simple to define. Its very nature and characteristics often lie beyond the limitations of words and the defined boundaries that words connote. However, definitions have been offered and characteristics common to mystical experiences have been listed by many philosophers, theologians, psychologists, and popular writers.

The etymology of the word itself is debated. Most agree that "mysticism" is derived from the Greek *mueo*—"to initiate," as in the mystery religions where the initiate takes a sacred oath to protect the secrets of the religion. Thus, the derivation may also come from *myein*, "to close the lips and eyes," referring either to the silence of the worshipper who stands before God or to the oath of the devotee not to reveal the sacred mysteries of the religion.

Evelyn Underhill wrote: "Mysticism, according to its historical and psychological definitions, is the direct intuition or experience of God; and a mystic is a person who has, to a greater or lesser degree, such a direct experience—one whose religion and life are centered, not merely on an accepted belief or practice, but on that which he regards as first hand personal knowledge."[1]

Georgia Harkness said that mysticism is "the direct and immediate awareness of the presence of God."[2] Somehow, the words "intuition of" or "experience of" or "awareness of" God do not seem adequate, for these words imply some distance between the knower and the known. The ultimate goal of the mystic is to achieve union with God, so that the self is lost

---

1. Underhill, *Mystics of the Church*, 9.
2. Harkness, *Mysticism*, 35.

The Mysticism of Ordinary and Extraordinary Experience

in the greater context of God. It is the participation of the soul in the life of God. And since the essence of God is love, the object of the mystic is the direct experience of the love of God.

Since the object of mysticism is "union with God," what this union means, or what happens when one achieves it, can have other ramifications such as the acquisition of knowledge inaccessible through normal perception or ordinary ways of knowing. Margaret Smith, in her study of the relation of Christian mysticism to the Islamic mysticism of the Sufis, says that the early mystics were true Gnostics whose goal was to rise above earthly knowledge to the contemplation of God and thereby gain through intuition an esoteric knowledge predestined for a chosen few who were found fit to receive it.[3] God was the Source of Knowledge and the Fountain of Wisdom to which the Gnostics aspired, but it was the later Christian mystics who sought God for God's own sake, for in not knowing, one knows and experiences God.

Mysticism is more often characterized not by knowing, but by feeling, and yet it is beyond emotion. The mystical state defies description, for mystical experiences cannot be confined to language since their very nature lies beyond the boundaries of words. The paradox seems to be that if one can talk about it, it's not a mystical experience. However, the literature of mysticism is monumental; mystics have found ways to talk about their experiences.

If we remember that the map is not the territory—that words are also symbols—we may begin to understand the nature of the mystical experience. As Hans Penner points out,

> [A]ll we have for understanding mysticism is language, not experience. It is not mystical experience which explains mystical traditions of languages; rather it is mystical language which explains mystical experience. In fact, it is useless to appeal to mystical experience as the basis of our explanation because it is precisely this experience that needs to be explained."[4]

Since language is the means that humans have developed to communicate knowledge and ideas, we can operate within that system as long as we understand its limitations.

The mystical way is one of three ways by which persons have sought to know God. In "natural theology," God is known through the created order. In "historical" and "dogmatic" theology, God is known through history,

---

3. Smith, *Way of the Mystics*, 1–2.
4. Penner, "Mystical Illusion," 91.

The Nature of Mystical Experiences

tradition, and the record of past revelation. Mystical theology is the soul's direct knowledge of God.[5] No one method of knowing God should stand alone. While the mystic may know immediately and intuitively, the experience must be compared to tradition to determine its validity.

Mysticism tends far more to confirm rather than question traditional authority. In an essay on "The Conservative Character of Mystical Experience," Steven Katz maintains that "Western mystics do not experience God in "neutral" or monistic ways [as suggested by W. T. Stace] and then interpret this experience for expediency's sake in theistic language, but rather, based on their prior study of canonical sources . . . , they have theistic and even more specifically, personal, intimate, theistic experiences."[6]

The mystic vision is framed within the context of the symbols and language that the mystic brings to the experience. God, so to speak, uses the tools in the mystic's own bag. Consequently, the teaching of the classical mystics was seen as either "(a) the older teachings in a new guise; (b) a personal confirmation of existing doctrine; (c) a legitimate extension of tradition teaching; or (d) a new, but authoritative, stage of tradition."[7] In a series of interviews that I conducted in the 1980s, I noticed that much of the symbolic language and descriptions that were received through dreams or other means were consistent with the cultural milieu of the percipient.

There is a question of subjectivity and objectivity in determining the criteria by which mystical experiences are judged. We can study the lives of the mystics, which Evelyn Underhill did exceptionally well, and elicit from that study characteristics held in common by those who have been accepted as mystics, recognizing that there are exceptions to the criteria, that not all mystics share the same characteristics in common. The alternative is to describe the mystical experience with a rigid set of criteria and hold each experience up to that yardstick. The problem is that in most cases all we have is the mystic's own story; third-person corroboration is extremely rare. In the past, the difference between madness and mysticism has rested with the acceptance of the community. Richard M. Bucke, a Canadian physician and author of *Cosmic Consciousness*, an early classic of mystical experience, wrote that "the first thing each person asks himself upon experiencing the new sense is: Does what I see and feel represent reality or

---

5. Underhill, *Mystics of the Church*, 14–15.
6. Katz, "The Conservative Character of Mystical Experience," 13.
7. Katz, "The Conservative Character of Mystical Experience," 22.

The Mysticism of Ordinary and Extraordinary Experience

am I suffering from a Delusion?"[8] Society has determined that the ability to distinguish between a shared reality and a personal reality is a measure of one's sanity. The validation of a mystical experience is therefore based on the individual's own report of that experience.

Following his own mystical experience of a flame-colored cloud engulfing him within his cab on his way home, Bucke undertook a comparative study of experiences and concluded his own list of characteristics and factors:

1. A "photism" or cosmic light, an inner illumination, either a sense of being immersed in it or the mind being filled with light.
2. Moral elevation, ecstasy, the assurance of "salvation."
3. Intellectual elevation, a clear conception of universal meaning, almost as a "gestalt."
4. A sense of immortality.
5. Loss of the fear of death.
6. Loss of the sense of sin.
7. Instantaneous illumination.
8. The moral character of the person prior to the experience is a factor.
9. Age. Bucke believed that maturity was a factor in attaining cosmic consciousness and that the average age for this maturity was thirty-five. Consequently, youthful experiences would have to be verified by the way in which a person lived following the experience.
10. The personality of the person. There is an added "charm" to the person who has attained cosmic consciousness; a certain charisma is noted in the bearing of such a person.
11. A change in the person following the experience such as profound joy or a "transfiguration"—or in Dante's terms a "transhumanization."[9]

Bucke's list has been criticized by W. T. Stace, who also took issue with William James' definitions (as well as D. T. Suzuki's list of common characteristics of *satori*) as too haphazard and lacking in correspondence.

William James, in the Gifford Lectures at Edinburgh in 1901–1902, proposed "four marks" of the mystical state of consciousness. These are:

8. Bucke, *Cosmic Consciousness*, 58.
9. Bucke, *Cosmic Consciousness*, 60–63.

The Nature of Mystical Experiences

(a) Ineffability—the impossibility of adequately describing the experiences which are "more like states of feeling than like states of intellect."[10] Words are insufficient vehicles of representation. One must experience it directly. It is like trying to understand love without ever being in love.

(b) Noetic quality—mystical states of consciousness are those in which awareness, revelation, knowledge, and insight are received by means other than normal perception or intellectual processes. James makes three points about this insight: it is extrasensory; it is of value; it is authoritative.

(c) Transiency—mystical states are of short duration. James estimated that the maximum would be about two hours with most experiences about a half hour in duration. My own experience, and those of persons I have interviewed, indicate that many of these experiences are momentary. They are also transitory in that they fade from consciousness as a dream fades the moment one's awareness is diverted to the normal routines of the day. However, the experience exists imperfectly in memory and can be recalled.

(d) Passivity—the mystical consciousness feels caught up by another power greater than itself. There is a suspension of the will and at times a sensation of separation from bodily consciousness. One is aware that one is not there, wherever "there" is or was. James connected this with certain "definite phenomena of secondary or alternative personality, such as prophetic speech, automatic writing, or the mediumistic trance."[11]

James said that the first two marks, ineffability and noetic quality, were not only essential but sufficient in defining mystical experiences, where the other two are "less sharply marked" but usually present.[12]

Evelyn Underhill found William James' four marks unsatisfactory and proposed four other tests for mystical experiences:

(a) Active and practical—the entire self is involved in the experience, not only the mind or intellect; it is participation and not merely reception.

(b) Transcendental and spiritual—the object of mysticism is God; not what God can give. The difference between magic and mysticism,

---

10. James, *Varieties of Religious Experience*, 293.
11. James, *Varieties of Religious Experience*, 293.
12. James, *Varieties of Religious Experience*, 381.

says Underhill, is that the object of magic is to get, while the object of mysticism is to give. The mystic does not seek occult wisdom or power, but only God.

(c) Love is the primary objective. This is the driving force of the mystic; it is the total dedication of the will which moves the soul to the Source of all love. This separates the true mystic experience, as far as Underhill is concerned, from merely paranormal experiences of the spiritual world.

(d) Living Union with the One—arrived at through the psychological and spiritual process known as the "Mystic Way."[13]

The classic mystical process involved purgation, illumination, and union. Underhill defined five stages of the mystic way. Since mystics may differ in what they bring, not all may be experienced by any one mystic, but most will vary between states of pleasure and states of pain. The states may be sharply defined, or they may be blurred and confused. These stages are:

1. The Awakening of the Self to Consciousness of Divine Reality—a well-defined experience of short duration usually accompanied by feelings of intense joy and exaltation or importance. This is the typical conversion experience that moves the person to a higher level of consciousness and greater awareness of God's presence.

2. The Purgation of the Self—the attempt to rid oneself of temptations and material desire through discipline and self-mortification as preparation to moving towards union with God. It is a state of pain and effort, a state of kenosis, of getting rid of the dross of the life, the impediments to unity.

3. Illumination—a state of apprehension of the Absolute, a sense of the Divine Presence. It is being blinded by the Light in order to see—the emergence from the cave of illusion to the knowledge of reality. It is a state of happiness and contemplation, but not true union. Many who have had mystic experiences never get beyond this state.

4. The Purification of the Self—the most terrible of mystic experiences, "mystic death" is the "dark night of the soul." It is the sense of divine dereliction, of cosmic abandonment. It is a second stage of *kenosis*, but whereas in Purgation the outward and material aspects of life are purged, here the self is emptied and prepared for surrender. If

---

13. Underhill, *Mysticism*, 81.

purgation is simply taking out the trash, purification is getting the house ready for the new owner.

5. Union—the ultimate goal of the mystic quest. It is not only a perception of the Absolute, but a merging, a becoming at one with the Divine. "It is a state of equilibrium, of purely spiritual life; characterized by peaceful joy, by enhanced powers, by intense certitude."[14] It is a state of ecstasy in which the mystic loses all awareness of the physical world and is satisfied with the contemplation and enjoyment of the divine vision. While states of ecstasy may appear in other stages, the state of union, which is the true goal of the mystic's progress, establishes a transcendent environment in which states of ecstasy "give a foretaste to the soul."[15]

Eastern mysticism goes one step beyond to a total annihilation of the self and a complete loss of identity of the person. In Western spirituality, union is the absorption of the self and complete surrender and subjection of the will to the Divine Will.

Underhill rejected the so-called "visions and voices" and other supernatural and paranormal phenomena as irrelevant to the mystical experience and maintained that any attempt "to identify mysticism with such forms and figures . . . is clearly wrong."[16]

Mysticism has always been associated with paranormal phenomena and even occult practices. Virtually all the mystics who have penetrated the veil separating the awareness of spiritual reality have exhibited paranormal abilities or reported "visions and voices." These may be the adiaphora of the mystical experience, but since they are so common and, as a sign, so representative of the mystical experience, they cannot be dismissed as irrelevant. They may not be the object of the mystical experience, but they are indicative of it.

W. T. Stace likewise dismissed the visions and voices and stated that even St. Paul's vision of the Christ on the Damascus road was not a mystical experience. While being subject to paranormal phenomena the mystics themselves discounted them as not important or of questionable value.

---

14. Underhill, *Mysticism*, 169–70, 176–443.
15. Underhill, *Mysticism*, 170.
16. Underhill, *Mysticism*, 79.

The Mysticism of Ordinary and Extraordinary Experience

Stace's reasoning is that the most important type of mystical experience is non-sensuous, while visions and voices use sensuous imagery.[17]

In characterizing mystical experiences, Stace first divided them into two classes: extrovertive mysticism and introvertive mysticism. The primary difference is that the former looks outward through the senses while the latter looks inward into the mind. Both attain the same goal of ultimate unity with the One. The characteristics of the extrovertive experience are:

1. The unifying vision, expressed abstractly by the formula "All is One." The One is, in extrovertive mysticism, perceived through the physical senses, in or through the multiplicity of objects.

2. The more concrete apprehension of the One as being an inner subjectivity in all things, described variously as life, or consciousness, or a living Presence. The discovery that nothing is "really" dead.

3. Sense of objectivity or reality.

4. Feeling of blessedness, joy, happiness, satisfaction, etc.

5. Feeling that what is apprehended is holy, or sacred, or divine. This is the quality which gives rise to the interpretation of the experience as being "of God." It is the specifically religious element in the experience. It is closely intertwined with, but not identical with, the previously listed characteristics of blessedness and joy.

6. Paradoxicality.

7. Alleged by mystics to be ineffable, incapable of being described in words, etc.[18]

Introvertive mysticism is universal and is attainable by anyone willing to enter a sensory deprivation tank or make use of other means to block out completely external stimuli and to eradicate all mental constructs, abstract thoughts, reasoning, or other mental content. What emerges is a state of pure consciousness—"pure in that it is not the consciousness of any empirical content. It has no content except itself."[19] In introvertive mysticism there is no sense of space or time, or of the self.

F. C. Happold, in his study of mysticism, accepted James' criteria and added three others. In addition to the Jamesian list of ineffability, noetic

---

17. Stace, *Mysticism and Philosophy*, 47–49.
18. Stace, *Mysticism and Philosophy*, 79.
19. Stace, *Mysticism and Philosophy*, 26.

The Nature of Mystical Experiences

quality, transiency, and passivity (to which is added "purgation"), there is the consciousness of the oneness of Everything, a sense of timelessness, and the conviction that the "ego" is not the "real"! (there is another "self," the "atman.")[20]

Rudolf Otto in his outstanding study of the numinous, *The Idea of the Holy*, sought to clarify the difference between rational religion and mystical religion. When we think of the Spirit of God by analogy to human reason and personality and apply the attributes of spirit, reason, purpose, good will, supreme power, unity, and selfhood, we are thinking of God conceptually. We have a God that can be grasped conceptually. This is the basis of rational religion from which belief ensues rather than feeling. Since language conveys ideas or concepts, religious truth expressed in language stresses the rational attributes of God. This is somewhat misleading since mysticism, its quality of ineffability notwithstanding, has resulted in an abundance of literature. The element that sets mystical religion apart from the rational is "the holy."[21]

Otto extracts from the meaning of "holy" a certain quality which he identifies as the numinous which is experienced outside of the self. When the numinous is experienced, there is a feeling of dependence, a submerging of "creature-consciousness" to "that which is supreme above all creatures."[22] The feeling of the numinous, the deepest and most fundamental element of religious emotion, is the *mysterium tremendum* which

> may at times come sweeping like a gentle tide, pervading the mind with a tranquil mood of deepest worship. It may pass over into a more set attitude of the so, continuing, as it were, thrillingly vibrant and resonant, until at last it dies away and the soul resumes its 'profane,' non-religious mood of everyday experience.[23]

The characteristics of the *mysterium tremendum* are:

(a) The element of awfulness, of dread, of holy fear (but not terror); the sense of being in the presence of inexpressible mystery.

(b) The element of majesty, of "overpoweringness," of absolute unapproachability; the sense of being in the presence of someone or something greater than oneself; of feeling one's "creaturehood."

20. Happold, *Mysticism*, 45–46.
21. Otto, *Idea of the Holy*, 1–5.
22. Otto, *Idea of the Holy*, 10.
23. Otto, *Idea of the Holy*, 12.

The Mysticism of Ordinary and Extraordinary Experience

(c) The element of energy, of urgency; of experiencing a force that is active, compelling and alive; it is the feeling of the consuming love of God or the scorching wrath of God, depending upon how the energy is directed."[24]

Otto offers the suggestion that in its first stage of development the religious consciousness began with the numen and took the form of "daemonic dread." The only form of worship that could result from this dread would be in the form of expiation or appeasement of the "wrath" of the numen. Further development led to the possession of the numen for its own sake resulting in the progression from asceticism to the development of the religious life to its consummation in the purest state of life in the spirit. Catherine of Genoa found these words to express it:

> O that I could tell you what the heart feels, how it burns and is consumed inwardly! Only, I find no words to express it. I can but say: Might one little drop of what I feel fall into Hell, Hell would be transformed into a Paradise.[25]

Finally, we turn to one of the more recent describers of mystical states of consciousness: the former radical Dominican priest Matthew Fox, whose introduction to creation spirituality in his book, *Original Blessing*, has created a new generation of mystics and incurred the displeasure of the Vatican in the process. Mysticism for Fox is resurrection, the raising of the human psyche to new levels of awareness of the wholeness of the creation. He offers a panentheistic God whose Spirit is alive in all things, and he sees a realized eschatology in terms of the reconciliation of creation to the Creator already at work in the Cosmic Christ whose Spirit is present now. Participation in the work of Christ is mysticism. According to Fox, everyone is a mystic, and by offering "twenty-one working, running, experiential definitions of mysticism," he hopes to elicit that mystical quality from each person. His list with a brief comment is as follows:[26]

1. Experience. The mystic must experience God (and life), not intellectualizing divinity, but rather, participating in it.
2. Nondualism. Mystical experiences are unitive, a bringing together of creation and of different existences.

---

24. Otto, *Idea of the Holy*, 13–14.
25. Otto, *Idea of the Holy*, 38.
26. Fox, *Coming of the Cosmic Christ*, 47–65.

The Nature of Mystical Experiences

3. Compassion. "The keen awareness of the interdependence of all living things which are all part of one another and involved in one another," as Thomas Merton said.
4. Connection Making. We connect with others in terms of experiences, stories, myths, music, form, and ritual. The artist as a maker of connections is a mystic.
5. Radical Amazement. To be in awe of, to marvel at, to stand in wonder of—"a reverential fear based on a realization of the greatness of our existence."
6. Affirmation of the World as a Whole. Gandhi described this as being "attuned to the whole of creation." It is participation in God's love for the world.
7. Right-Brain. The physiological locus of mystical ability and the lobe responsible for synthesis and creativity.
8. Self-Critical. Self-examination and the avoidance of the internalization of self-hatred. This is also seen as a willingness to criticize religion.
9. Heart Knowledge. A trust in the experience of the heart. The psychiatrist Otto Rank said that when the irrational and mystical is repressed, it will emerge as personal neurosis or cultural violence.
10. A Return to the Source. Mysticism is what "religion" originally meant—"a binding back or bonding" with our source.
11. Feminist. Letting go of patriarchal consciousness and seeing creation—the cosmic mother—as simply being.
12. Panentheistic. "All things in God and God in all things."
13. Birthing Images. The use of images, the gift of the artist, in understanding spiritual realities.
14. Silence. "We embrace silence in order to experience being." It is that suspended moment when one arrives at the source of one's being and becomes aware of that power from words derive. It is the silent moment of creation.
15. Nothingness and Darkness. Experiencing pain and doubt—the "dark night of the soul."
16. Childlike Playfulness. Getting rid of accumulated baggage and inhibitions and being eager to play and indulge in fantasy.

17. Psychic Justice. Righteousness or internalized justice. Social injustice is rooted in personal injustice and vice versa. The mystic's search for internal peace moves him or her to work for global peace.
18. Prophetic. The mystic must be prophetic; mysticism is not total withdrawal but movement into the social arena.
19. Being-With-Being. Identification and "at-one-ment" with the suffering, the victims of injustice and oppression, and absorbing the hatred and pain of others.
20. True Self. The unleashing of the inner person, the true self which is a mirror of divinity.
21. Globally Ecumenical. Mysticism is the unleashing of power from all the world's religions; a universalism that calls for the rising above caste or creed.

Matthew Fox uses the above categories to define mysticism but offers seven tests to discern their authenticity. They are justice, the intellectual life, paradox and humor (the recognition of the diversity of things and the omnipresence of divinity), fertility (mysticism bears fruit), unselfconsciousness, dialectical consciousness (the ability to embrace the "both/and instead of settling for the dualistic either/ors"), and the ability to experience the Cosmic Christ in all things.

Fox's characteristics represent a new approach to an interpretation of the classical mystical experience and may be useful to those who are seeking the mystic way. The most important and most desired of these characteristics is participation in the experience of God which alters one's perspective so that all of life is seen as a totality. This awareness of the interconnectedness of all things often produces a feeling of compassion for people and their environment and a desire for social and ecological justice. The awareness of God's presence most often has an effect on a person's worldview.

The Conscious Universe

In the beginning when God created the heavens and the earth, the earth was a formless void and darkness covered the face of the deep, while a wind from God swept over the face of the waters.
Then God said, "Let there be light"; and there was light. And God saw that the light was good; and God separated the light from the darkness. God called the light Day, and the darkness he called Night. And there was evening and there was morning, the first day.
—GENESIS 1:1–5

In the beginning was the Word, and the Word was with God, and the Word was God. He was in the beginning with God. All things came into being through him, and without him not one thing came into being. What has come into being in him was life, and the life was the light of all people.
—JOHN 1:1–4

Once Jesus was asked by the Pharisees when the kingdom of God was coming, and he answered, "The kingdom of God is not coming with things that can be observed; nor will they say, 'Look, here it is!' or 'There it is!' For, in fact, the kingdom of God is among you."
—LUKE 17:20–21

He is the image of the invisible God, the firstborn of all creation; for in him all things in heaven and on earth were created, things visible and invisible, whether thrones or dominions or rulers or powers—all things have been created through him and for him. He himself is before all things, and in him all things hold together.
—COLOSSIANS 1:15–17

The Mysticism of Ordinary and Extraordinary Experience

GENESIS DOESN'T REALLY START at the beginning. It assumes the existence of a formless void, wind, and water. And of course, it assumes the existence of God which or who it does not define. When Genesis records, "Then God *said*," it is not referring to sound, for to whom would God speak? It is a matter of thought or will or consciousness that decrees the existence of the electro-magnetic spectrum of which sound and light are part.

St. John begins his Gospel: "In the beginning was the Word." There is a similar expression in Tibet: "In the beginning was OM," the cosmic vibration that is to merge sound into substance. In the book of Genesis, the first word spoken by God is light. The word "light," as well as the English "loud" and the Greek *logos* (which means both "sound" and "word") all go back to the same root, *leg*. This is one of the primal words of our language. From it are derived the words for light, lamp, law, language, and religion. (*lux*—light, *logos*, *lychne*—lamp, *lex*—law, language, *legein*—to collect or hold together, which is the Latin root of *re-ligio*, religion.) So light and sound and logos and religion are all on the same wavelength.[1]

The way we compose language and use words reflects how we think.

When God speaks, the sound or word becomes the thing itself, becoming the substance of its own energy. It is sound that brings down the walls of Jericho. It is sound that accompanies the presence of God as the ark is brought to Jerusalem (2 Sam 6:15). In the Old Testament, silence was used to indicate death or the perception of the absence of God, but sound—loud sound—usually indicated God's presence. When Elijah was on Mount Horeb, the scriptures say that God was not in the earthquake, wind, and fire, but in "the sound of sheer silence" (1 Kgs 19:12). Even in silence there is sound; even in death there is life; even when God seems absent, God's presence is there. The Apostle Paul says that there are many different sounds in the world, "and nothing is without sound" (1 Cor 4:10). We need to know the meaning of sound that we may interpret God (1 Cor 14:10–11). So, from a scientific point of view, this energy, light, sound, and more pervades the universe. Thought always precedes action, even on a subconscious level. The word becomes flesh; thought becomes matter.

From a faith perspective, it is God that is in all things. Many religions recognize *panentheism*, literally "God in all," since all things are created and held together by this atomic energy. This is nothing new. It can be traced back through Spinoza to Plotinus and Neoplatonism. The universe is contained within the consciousness of God, and God pervades all things.

---

1. Berendt, *World Is Sound*, 52.

This is also an aspect of Incarnation where the presence of the Divine is in all people and clearly evident in certain religious leaders such as Jesus of Nazareth.

On the Pfahler Hall of Science at Ursinus College are engraved the words of the astronomer Johannes Kepler who said, "O, Almighty God, I am thinking Thy thoughts after Thee!" It is another way of saying that humans have access to divine consciousness.

Ken Wilber, a very prolific author who wrote *The Spectrum of Consciousness* and *The Holographic Paradigm*, which examines the intersection of scientific and religious explanations of the world, reminds us that none of the founders of the world's great religions handed down myths. They all had a direct experience of God and that mystical experiences do meet the criteria for the scientific method.

Sir John Polkinghorne, the eminent particle physicist and Anglican priest, spoke at Lancaster Theological Seminary. In the course of his presentation on "A New Natural Theology," he referred frequently to the "mind of God." Simply put, the object of natural theology is to comprehend the nature of God through reason rather than revelation, or at least understand revelation through reason. Polkinghorne's new natural theology is to see the mind of God behind the laws of nature and scientific explanation. Apart from God's many incarnations in human form, through which divine revelation must be apprehended by faith, one was left wondering how mind can exist in a nonphysical state.

I asked Sir John about the mind existing apart from the body. I had hoped that he would reply from his background in subatomic particles, the realm of quarks, hadrons, baryons and mesons, and ultimately super string theory, whereby the nature of the material universe is reduced to vibrations of energy. Instead, Polkinghorne responded by saying that in the afterlife we will be given a different body, a spiritual body. The implication seemed to be that the mind needs some sort of vehicle in order to be able to operate.

How does pure thought function? Is God the collective unconscious (as in Carl Jung's concept), a nonspecific, ubiquitous, nondescript process? When it comes to the exosomatic human mind, was Sir John suggesting that there is a need for a localized, differentiated mind that maintained some spatial identity? How else could apparitions appear in a particular place, at a particular time, to a particular person or group of persons? Or is the apparition dependent upon the mind of the perceiver being processed

The Mysticism of Ordinary and Extraordinary Experience

by a physical brain. Do spiritual entities manifest themselves when there is no perceiver present?

The parapsychologist would say, "Of course they do. And we have electronic voice phenomena, light impressions on photographic plates, videotape, and more to *prove* it." (Of course, the question of what is "proof" is subject to debate.)

I found myself at the conclusion of Sir John Polkinghorne's presentation saying with C. S. Lewis, "Your God is too small." The mind and intelligence of God are beyond our comprehension and the ability of a finite brain to process. As much as I enjoy probing the mysteries of science and spirituality, I delight in being in awe of mystery and wonder. I will stretch my mind to its limits while acknowledging that there is ever so much beyond it. Is it possible that there are other ways of knowing, of comprehending our reality (or a different one), that is beyond our cause and effect logic?

The God of the Bible is continually asking humans to "repent" (in Greek, *metanoia*, literally "to change one's mind"). Those who refuse to accept a reality other than their own creation are said to have *paranoia*, "mind beside itself." Perhaps there is a greater need for *exonoia*, "mind beyond itself." What really is wrong with occasionally being out of one's mind?

It may be helpful every now and then to stretch our minds as we explore that which lies beyond the veil of our physical lives. The nature of consciousness, the concept of the continuing self, empirical data in survival research, and more, should be examined from a variety of perspectives. This includes artificial intelligence. Not only will machines created by humans develop intelligence and the ability to process algorithms, but will they also be able to develop consciousness whereby they become aware of themselves?

A term is that gaining in popularity these days is "panpsychism." In an article on rock consciousness by Olivia Goldhill,[2] she refers to Philip Goff, philosophy professor at Central European University in Budapest, Hungary, who says that "Panpsychism offers an attractive alternative solution: Consciousness is a fundamental feature of physical matter; every single particle in existence has an "unimaginably simple" form of consciousness. These particles then come together to form more complex forms of consciousness, such as humans' subjective experiences. This isn't meant to imply that particles have a coherent worldview or actively think, merely

---

2. Goldhill, "Everything from Spoons to Stones."

that there's some inherent subjective experience of consciousness in even the tiniest particle."[3]

Edmund W. Sinnott, a biologist writing in the 1950s, examined the biological evidence for the existence of the human spirit and suggested that even one-celled life forms may have consciousness. In his book, *Cell and Psyche*, he used the term *telism* and argued that mind and matter are two aspects of the same phenomenon and that purpose exists in all organisms as it is built into the genotype and the protoplasm.[4]

The writer of John's Gospel may have had quantum insight when he said, "In the beginning was the Word, and the Word was with God, and the Word was God. He was in the beginning with God. All things came into being through him, and without him not one thing came into being. What has come into being in him was life, and the life was the light of all people" (John 1:1–5).

The Word, *logos*, also means in Greek the inner thought or consciousness. Incidentally, the words *conscious* and *science* contain the same Latin root *"scio,"* meaning "to know." So a question that might arise is whether consciousness is a problem of physics or of faith.

There are questions that science cannot answer. It may tell us *how*, but not *why*.

Why is there something instead of nothing?

Why is there evil in the world?

Why do we exist?

What happens to "us," meaning the individual consciousness, after death or the destruction of the Universe?

One of the elusive frontiers between science and faith is what is called "paranormal." Many of these incidents are recorded in the Bible and come under the heading of "miracles," Latin for "small wonders." I have already mentioned apparitions. What are they?—"false creations of the heat-oppressed brain" (2.1), as Shakespeare's Macbeth conjectured. History is filled with such reported sightings. Or Near-Death Experiences, consciousness beyond the body that has been studied by many physicians and other respected scientists. If consciousness can exist beyond the physical, can this explain the concept of reincarnation that is believed by much of the world's population? Premonitions seem to be distortions of the space-time

---

3. Goldhill, "Everything from Spoons to Stones."
4. Glass, "Cell and Psyche," 62.

The Mysticism of Ordinary and Extraordinary Experience

continuum, but occur with such frequency that invites new inquiries into our understanding of time.

The paranormal has traditionally been regarded by many scientists as non-legitimate or "pseudo-science" and has largely been ignored or dismissed because most of these incidents are not replicable and cannot be studied by accepted empirical methodology.

However, within the last fifty years, respected scientists such as Charles Tart have reconciled the scientific and spiritual worlds by looking at empirical evidence that points to our spiritual nature. I would invite you to consider his book, *The End of Materialism—How Evidence of the Paranormal Is Bringing Science and Spirit Together*. Dr. Tart is on the Advisory Council of an organization of which I was president and continue to serve on its board: The Academy of Spirituality and Consciousness Studies.

Science and Faith are considering all aspects of existence but are asking different questions and using different methods of knowing, but in the end it will come together. In the Invisible God, all things hold together.

Things That Go Bump in the Night

AN OLD SCOTTISH PRAYER petitions the deity: "From ghoulies and ghosties and long leggety beasties, and things that go bump in the night, Good Lord, deliver us!"

There is no question that the phenomena of the appearances of the dead in the form of discarnate spirits have been part of the record of human civilization since antiquity. Ever since Neanderthals buried their dead painted with red ochre facing the rising sun and provided them with a travel kit for the afterlife, there has been a persistent belief in the survival of human consciousness in some form or another. The visitations of ghosts and spiritual entities have been a part of many of the world's religions, cultural mythology, and as a literary device in the literature of many societies.

Shakespeare, for example, living in a period when ghosts, witches, and demons were a part of the cultural landscape, has ghostly visitations in three of his greatest tragedies—Hamlet, Macbeth, and Julius Caesar—each of which are used as a literary device to seek justice or provide information, a common reason given for such manifestations.

The belief in the existence of ghosts is as varied from society to society and in different time periods. When I conducted my own research in the mid-1980s, 26 percent of those who responded to my survey indicated that they had seen or sensed a person known to have been dead.

Exactly what is a ghost? Is it something out there that can affect the sensory apparatus of the percipient? Is it the electromagnetic residue of deceased persons posited in the new science of ghosts? Is it the result of biochemical malfunction or aberrant neuro-electric stimulation of the brain? Or is it as Ebenezer Scrooge suggested, when confronted by the spirit of Jacob Marley, the result of "an undigested bit of beef, a blot of mustard, a crumb of cheese, a fragment of an underdone potato?"

The Mysticism of Ordinary and Extraordinary Experience

Do we believe in ghosts—spirits of the dead—because we cannot believe in our own nonexistence, which is part of the evolutionary self-preservation and ego-defense mechanism? Or is there something in every culture down through recorded time that presents sufficient reason to accept the validity of apparitions and other paranormal activity?

In attempting to define what a "ghost" is, we can look at it etymologically. "Ghost" is derived from the Old English word *gast*, meaning "breath" or "spirit." It is akin to the German *geist* which has a multiplicity of meanings. The Bible refers to *ruach* which is the "breath" of God, breathed into Adam at the Creation, so that humans possess an element of the Divine. The biblical expression for dying in the King James Version is "to give up the ghost." Jesus' final act on the cross was to "release his pneuma" or spirit. At the time of physical death, this "ruach-geist-spirit-ghost" returns to its source. But sometimes it doesn't, and occasionally, it makes its presence felt among those who are in physical existence, and for some reason, it desires to communicate with us.

The concept of ghosts can be traced back to the Pyramid Texts of ancient Egypt where a prayer to Hathor, prayed while drinking beer, was said as a protection from vengeful spirits. The Egyptians believed that at death the *ka*, the spiritual shell of the person, would be detached from the body. The *ka* could travel and be seen by living persons in the form of a ghost. It was necessary, therefore, for pyramids and tombs, called *het-ka*, or "house of the ka," to have spirit doors to allow the ka to escape and to return as it needed. A more recent variation of this is the *seelen fenster* of the Pennsylvania Germans, built into their houses to permit the soul or spirit to depart at death.

The Egyptian influence on the religion of the Hebrews during their sojourn in the land of the Pharaohs has been underestimated. Egyptian polytheism, which embraced the deities of the Canaanite and surrounding cultures, stood in marked contrast to Hebrew monotheism. However, one cannot help but speculate that since the children of Abraham were living in Egypt during the Amarna period when Akhenaton was worshiping the Creator God, Aton, that Yahweh's revelation to Moses on Horeb might be a natural progression. The similarities between Aton and Yahweh are extensive.

The Egyptian view of the afterlife was certainly much more complex and highly convoluted compared to that of the Hebrews. Unlike the Egyptians, the Hebrews in the pre-exilic period had little concept of the afterlife.

Death was the final state of existence, and that was all that it was—simply being, with no sense of animation or purpose.

In what many scholars believe to be the earliest of the Hebrew creation stories, (there are fragments of Babylonian creation stories in Pss 74:14; 89:10; Job 41:1), Genesis 2:4b–7, God scooped up the primal mud, fashioned it into the human form, and "breathed into his nostrils the breath of life; and the man became a living being" (Gen 2:7). Like the potter-God, Khoum, Yahweh creates life (see also Jer 18:6) from the earth. The word used for "living being" or "soul" is the word *nephesh*. According to Edmond Jacob, the *nephesh* is the usual term for man's total nature whose defining characteristic is breath (*ruach*).[1] When the *ruach* leaves the body the *nephesh* is diminished, but when the *nephesh* leaves the body, the person is dead, and the *nephesh* ceases to exist.

However, there was a persistent belief that it was possible for the spirit or ghost to be summoned from its abode in *Sheol*. It is likely that the idea of *Sheol* was appropriated by the Hebrews from their Canaanitic neighbors who had a mystical relationship with the natural world and believed in several deities, chief of which was Ba'al, a dying-rising storm god. The etymology of *Sheol* seems to derive from the Hebrew word meaning "to ask or inquire," and in a cognitive form from the Akkadian *sa ilu*, "one who consults spirits."[2] This helps us to understand the encounter of King Saul with the medium of Endor (1 Sam 28), a Canaanitic earth-based shaman, who was asked to conjure the spirit of Samuel so that Saul might ask of the dead what he is to do. Necromancy was practiced by the Canaanites but forbidden by the Hebrews since it was outside of the normal priestly channels of discerning the will of God. Samuel is brought up from *Sheol*, which in this context is the place from which oracles are derived. The medium was called an *obh*, but she is also said to possess an *obh* which is a familiar spirit who aids in the conjuring of entities. The *obh* is a revenant, one who returns to earth after death.

This is not the only time that ghosts are mentioned in Biblical literature. In Matthew 14:26, the disciples having seen Jesus walking upon the sea were troubled saying, "It is an apparition and cried out in fear." The Greek word used here is "phantasm," meaning an "image presented to the mind by an object." The King James Version says that the disciples believed

---

1. Jacob, *Theology of the Old Testament*, 160.
2. Gaster, "Abode of the Dead," 788.

The Mysticism of Ordinary and Extraordinary Experience

that they saw a "spirit." Regardless of what actually did transpire, the disciples and others believed that a spirit could manifest itself.

Matthew (27:52–53) says that at the time of Jesus' death, "the tombs also were opened, and many bodies of the saints who had fallen asleep were raised. After his resurrection they came out of the tombs and entered the holy city and appeared to many." Whether these are physical bodies restored to life or spiritual entities that appeared is subject to interpretation, although early Christians did believe in a bodily resurrection. However, Jesus' non-physical body is said to materialize and dematerialize, and to move through walls. But Jesus denies that he is a ghost in Luke 24:39, saying that a spirit (*pneuma*) does not have flesh and bones. He also is able to sit down to dinner as he did on the road to Emmaus—and then disappears before paying the bill. He also attended a breakfast barbecue on the beach, which raises the question as to whether ghosts have physical needs (as the Egyptians believed when they provided snacks for the dead). Or was this merely a perception on the part of the believers?

Thus, the New Testament scriptures, while indicating that there was a belief in the existence of ghosts or spirits or phantasms, makes the point that the resurrected Jesus is of a different substance. It also raises the question as to whether it is possible for ghosts to possess some degree of corporeality, or are they entirely spectral images that impress the brain, bypassing the usual sensory network?

To a certain extent, believing is seeing. In those periods of human history when the belief in ghosts was most popular, the incidence of reports of sightings was correspondingly higher. Likewise, the appearance of ghosts and apparitions seem to conform to the needs and beliefs current in the particular age. Ghosts in the Classical age, for example, are able to see into the future and make predictions or offer advice to the living. Medieval ghosts looked paler and sadder than previous ghosts and seemed to give evidence of post-mortem suffering. This worked well for a church that was developing its theology of purgatory and sought to use apparitions to justify its system of punishment and reward. These ghosts literally served to scare the hell out of those considering a departure from the church's teachings. During the period of the Enlightenment, when Deism and scientific inquiry were in ascendance, the reported sightings of ghosts diminished. Ghosts experienced a resurgence during the Victorian period and saw the creation in 1882 of the Society for Psychical Research which sought to collect and evaluate the ghostly appearances of dying persons. An extensive study of ghosts in western culture through history can be found in *Ghosts: Appearances of the Dead and Cultural Transformation* by Ronald C. Finucane.

Hans Holzer, parapsychologist and author of more than 120 books on the paranormal, distinguished between ghosts and spirits saying that ghosts are related to a particular place associated with the person's death or a place with which they had close association in this life. Ghosts are usually the spirits of persons who have suffered a traumatic death and are confused as to where they are, often not realizing that they have passed through the veil of death. Generally, ghosts do not travel but haunt a particular location. Spirits have purpose and may appear to comfort, to reassure, to convey information, to seek fulfillment or resolution of an issue.

I was once called into a case involving a girl whose death occurred under mysterious circumstances. Although the authorities classified her death as natural, all other evidence, including postmortem forensic analysis, indicated a homicide. The parents of the girl reported that shortly after her death they began experiencing signs of her presence in their home (although she hadn't lived there for several years)—the smell of her perfume, movement of objects, non-aural communication, feeling of other entities in the house. I also felt the girl's presence on the stairs.

On a subsequent visit, a well-known psychic corroborated as much. The parents said that they had had the same experience and that their dog would also respond to something on the steps. There were additional signs that there was something unconventional about the situation.

Our sense of what was happening is that the deceased girl desired to comfort her family, to relay information that would afford closure, so that she and her parents could move on.

Ghosts, of course, have a mind of their own, as do we all, and we need to at least entertain the possibility of their existence and their desire to communicate with us. After all, as Hamlet said to his friend: "There are more things in heaven and earth, Horatio, than are dreamt of in your philosophy" (1.5).

Ghosts are as varied as the personalities they represent, but several characteristics emerge. They seem to be more concerned about their own personal issues relating to themselves and those close to them. They don't seem to be worried about politics and affairs of state.

Usually ghosts are attached to a particular place associated with them. Even the stories of the phantom hitchhiker that comes out of the Carolinas

The Mysticism of Ordinary and Extraordinary Experience

expresses the desire to return home. These are among the strangest and most enduring of ghost stories.

A man driving along a deserted road at night sees a young girl walking alone by the side of the road. He offers her a ride to the next city where she says she lives. En route, they engage in conversation though the girl seems somewhat distracted. She gives the driver her address, and upon their arrival he stops the car to let her out, but discovers that there is no one there. The man goes up to the house and knocks on the door and asks the woman who answers if she knows the young girl he describes to her. The woman knows all too well. The passenger is her daughter who had been killed in an automobile accident while on her way home. Many times, she had tried to come home, but always vanished when she arrived. The man can hardly believe the story, for his passenger was as real to him as anyone could be.

What I like about this story is that it dispels the idea that ghosts are only incorporeal phantasms that one perceives out of the corner of one's eye, but upon closer scrutiny disappear into the shadows. While certainly the transparent, vaporous type of ghost is more typical in legend, there are many cases where men and women engage in conversation with persons that are later found to be no longer of this life.

Over the years I have interviewed many persons who claim that they have experienced the presence of deceased loved ones in their homes. Often there are non-visual signs, but occasionally there are sightings. In attempting to verify the authenticity of these appearances, I want to make sure that what the person claims to see is not a product of the mind, a wish-fulfilling hallucination. I look for the corroboration of others who may have had witnessed the same phenomena. A basic question is why persons feel that they have had this communication, or what the apparition is seeking to communicate. Often, when the percipient feels that they know why they have seen a ghost and understand the so-called ghost's intentions, the sightings cease.

The question remains: Are ghosts the false creations of the percipient's brain, as Macbeth pondered, or are they entities from a spiritual world that can appear to many persons who can corroborate the sightings? Should we relegate the stories to Halloween fantasies or continue to explore a dimension of being so different from our present reality? The world is filled with mysteries yet to be discovered.

Episodes in the Life of a House

IF A HOUSE LIVES long enough, it will accumulate its share of ghosts, those spirits of its former tenants who have grown so attached to their earthly life that they refuse to be evicted by death.

As in life, the spirits who remain on this earth have different personalities. There are those who are angry and vindictive, resentful of the living that have moved into their home and now occupy the physical space that was so familiar to them. There are those who have some unfinished agenda, whose only mission is to bring to completion what they tried to do while they walked the earth. A few are there to impart some information, to correct the history of the past and set straight some divergent thinking. There are some suicides among these entities who feel they have been misunderstood. There is also the mischievous group who just likes to have some fun with the living, bedeviling them for the sport of it. They wish no harm but seek only their own amusement.

By far, the largest group of spiritual entities who manifest themselves are those confused and lost souls who wander around aimlessly looking for some direction and guidance. They are now as they were when they lived in this world, beings that drift with the flow and go wherever life would take them. They chart no course, seek no star, and carry no anchor. They stumble around in the spiritual world trying to find some direction, unable to move toward the source of all that is.

Sometimes when the living appears to sense their presence, these phantasms rush to attract attention to establish some communication link to the physical world. Like a door that has opened just a crack in a darkened room, allowing a sliver of light to shine through, these spirits congregate at the opening and do what they may to let those physical beings know of their existence.

The Mysticism of Ordinary and Extraordinary Experience

These spirits may be compared to a man who was trying to train a very stubborn mule and was not very successful at it. After exhausting all of the resources at his disposal, he took the reluctant mule to a farmer who had quite a reputation for training animals. Upon agreeing to the terms for the mule's education, the farmer picked up a sledgehammer and slammed the animal between the eyes, knocking him instantly to the ground. "What did you do that for?" asked the equally stunned owner. Said the farmer: "Before I can teach that mule anything, I must first get his attention."

While the spirits seek to arouse our interest with their paranormal behavior, it is also true that our eyes must first be opened in order to see. And sometimes one must see in order to understand. For me, this occasion did not come in one transforming event, but rather in a series of inexplicable, though minor occurrences, while living in an old farmhouse in Northampton County, Pennsylvania.

The house has an interesting history. Built in the middle of the nineteenth century with an addition during the 1920s, the farmhouse was a veritable stone fortress. It had been owned by a lawyer, Robert James, who became the district attorney for Northampton County and made an unsuccessful bid for the United States Congress. As district attorney, James undoubtedly was responsible for sending a goodly number of men and women to prison for assorted crimes. According to the local stories that were still being circulated in the 1960s, James had a fear bordering on paranoia that someday one of the convicted felons would attempt to gain revenge. Consequently, James fortified the house. There was a double set of windows for the interior and exterior of the house, and iron bars installed on the downstairs windows. An iron gate formed part of the triple door entry, and the grounds were quite well illuminated for a house of the 1920s. Built to withstand siege, there was a redundancy of the basic facilities to operate a home: water supplied by both spring and well, heat supplied by oil-heated hot air and coal-heated steam, electrical service, and backup generator. There were hidden compartments in the basement where we were told extra provisions could be stored. I suppose it might be considered reasonable to be prepared for any emergency when living in an isolated rural location. However, the house itself, when considered with the stories that were circulating about Robert James, left one wondering.

In retrospect, I am not certain whether I knew about Mr. James and his quirky behavior prior to the strange experiences which we encountered or if the bits and pieces of information came to light as we shared our stories among the congregation I served as pastor. In either case, the events themselves seemed unrelated to James' personality traits.

We lived in the house for three years, but within an eight-month period a number of unexplained events took place. Each one of them in and of themselves might have a rational explanation, or be attributable to imagination, or even faulty recollection, but the number of events and the number of various relatives and visitors that experienced them has caused me to speculate whether some other forces might be at work.

The earliest recollection is that of an incident that occurred to my wife, Mary Ann, who was home alone during the day. She had carried the laundry up from the basement and had set it on the kitchen table while she answered the phone. As she looked back, she saw, for a fraction of a second, the basket of laundry seemingly hovering in the air at the top of the stairs. And then, just as suddenly, it was propelled down the steps.

On another occasion she had taken her laundry outside to hang it on the line. When she tried to reenter the house, she found the door locked, and all the other doors locked, including doors that were normally kept open. When I returned home, I found her outside. I unlocked the front door and went in and checked the back door that she had been using. Not only was the door locked, but the deadbolt had been thrown, an action which requires a deliberate force from someone acting within the house.

Various noises were heard from time to time. A throbbing heartbeat type sound would emanate from a particular section of wall where there were no heating vents. The doorbell would ring with no apparent cause. This resulted in a somewhat humorous incident which enhanced the reputation of the house as haunted. We had called in an electrician to check the circuitry and locate the reason for the ringing. As he stood in the hall ready to leave, he told us that he could not find any reason for the bell to ring, that perhaps it was our imagination or that someone was playing a trick on us. At that very moment, the doorbell rang and there was no one there.

Sitting in the downstairs living room, we would occasionally hear the sound of footsteps upstairs, as though someone was moving about in bare feet. The animals would sometimes react in fear—the dog would bark; the cat would hiss and circle a bare spot on the floor.

Although the house was well-heated, there was one spot in the hall that was always cold, even in summer, though the surrounding air was warm, defying whatever I had read about thermodynamics. This did not bother us at all until one hot and steamy August morning. Mary Ann was lying in bed in the hours before dawn, trying to get some sleep in the unusually oppressive heat. She extended her arm beyond the bed and felt a dry, cold spot that contrasted sharply with the sultry atmosphere in the rest of the room. As she moved her hand about, in and out of the atmosphere fluctuation, she could discern the shape of a human figure. It departed very abruptly.

Whatever it was that was in the house, if it was anything at all, was not malicious. Although we were frightened at times, we never felt threatened. In fact, on one particular day Mary Ann and I were appreciative of the help that was rendered. It was late afternoon in early fall, shortly after our son was born. We had put Stuart to bed about four o'clock and had gone downstairs to the living room. We must have been so engrossed in our reading that we didn't realize the passage of time, nor the fact that the temperature had changed and become quite cold. Mary Ann immediately went upstairs to take a blanket out to cover Stuart. She was surprised to find that the baby was neatly covered, an impossible feat for a two-month-old infant. We were just as certain that neither one of us had covered the child earlier.

There were incidents that might be termed psychokinetic in nature. One morning all the curtain rods on the downstairs windows simply fell with no apparent cause. We returned home one evening to find every light in the house turned on, from the basement to the attic, including the closet lights. We had left during the afternoon, so we are reasonably certain that most, if not all, of the lights were off. There was no sign of entry or anything missing. Sometimes, a weighted sash cord could be seen swinging in a bathroom window in such an arc that would be impossible unless it had been deliberately set in motion. On another occasion, an overnight guest heard the sound of a cranking noise about three o'clock in the morning which she attributed to my working late on an old mimeograph machine. I assured her that I had retired at twelve and had not been using the machine prior to that.

One afternoon the animals were especially terrified. The dog was cringing in one corner of the dining room, the cat hissing in another. Mary Ann came downstairs to see what the problem was and was overcome by a strong sense of fear. She immediately left the house and went to the home of a nearby friend. The friend's teenage daughter agreed to return and spend the night. That night was also very warm, and the girl opened both the inside and outside windows and decided to sit in the space between the two windows to get some air. She had been sitting in the two-and-a-half-foot space when both the outside and inside windows closed simultaneously, trapping her in the wall. Her cries alerted Mary Ann who with some difficulty, eventually extricated her.

As the experiences began to accumulate, we tried to learn more about the history of the house. Some said that it may have been used as a way station on the Underground Railroad and that there was a secret room in the basement. We never found one, though the basement was such a forboding place that we seldom went to the back part of the cellar. The previous tenants kept pretty much to themselves, although the woman had mentioned to her neighbors that she never felt at ease in that house.

Years later, after we had moved from that parish, we learned that the subsequent owners had experienced at least two incidents: the sound of their piano playing in the middle of the night, and the sudden collapse of all their wall hangings on the first floor. They did not stay long in the house.

Several years ago, I visited the current owners of the house and asked them about any unusual experiences. They had none and were surprised to learn of the house's history.

The experiences in this house near Martins Creek were the sledgehammer that opened my eyes to the possibility that there is more to the human experience that reason can explain. The questions were endless: Was all of this a product of a shared imagination? Were there unearthly forces at work operating on their own? Was our attention deliberately being sought? Was the house infused with the presence of Robert James, or some residual energy or personality of a previous owner? Were these events the results of an impersonal force, or were they caused by someone or something motivated by purpose or design? Did the house's proximity to the cemetery cause it to be a gathering place for earthbound spirits looking for help? Was I, as a new pastor, perceived as some sort of spiritual intermediary who could give direction to those who had passed on, even as I was expected to guide those who were still present in the flesh?

This was the beginning of my personal search for a context or paradigm to make sense of my own experiences, and the experiences of those shared with me by church members who also sought explanations for what we are now calling paranormal events. If the events are indeed real, as they are believed to be by the percipients, then they ought to fit into a belief structure in which they can be interpreted and dealt with. If they are simply mental constructs, their psychological origins need to be explored and a hypothesis made for their seemingly pervasive occurrence throughout history, literature, and especially religion.

The Mysticism of Ordinary and Extraordinary Experience

Even after leaving the Martins Creek area, similar experiences continued to affect my family and myself. In my new church, we often felt unseen presences watching over us, and sometimes impressing us with thoughts that were not our own. When my young daughter came running to me, terrified at having seen a tall, dark-skinned man with feathers in his hair, I had no explanation for her except to dismiss it as imagination.

I had an occasion to share in the "imagination," or maybe it was a hallucination, of two church members shortly before they died. Marvin was a cancer patient in the Reading Hospital. During one of my visits, as I entered the room, I heard Marvin engaged in conversation with an empty chair. He introduced me to his brother and continued to talk to the unseen presence, occasionally turning to me so as not to leave me out. I played along with this charade and wondered whether I was in the presence of a spiritual being, or a part of Marvin's hallucination. The experience was open to several possible interpretations.

Katie was also dying, but she didn't know it—or she didn't want to admit it. I visited her in the morning of the day before Christmas. She told me that she had had a dream during the night in which she saw her previously departed brother standing at the door of the kitchen, across the room from where she had been sleeping. He had never before appeared to her in a dream or other manifestation. In fact, she said she had not even thought about him for years. But there he was smiling at her. He said only, "I'll see you soon," and was gone. Katie died the evening of the next day.

Was this an actual appearance of a spiritual being from another dimension of existence or the product of Katie's subconscious mind attempting to deal with her body's deterioration? Or was there some other explanation?

Though I was ordained to be a practitioner of the Christian faith, an interpreter of the Gospel of Jesus Christ, and a steward of the mysteries of God, I found myself confronted with mysteries that I could not interpret. I even questioned whether they were properly within the realm of my calling. Yet, people were having these experiences and raising questions about them in the context of their religious faith, and I was finding that the church, in its current expression of its theology and faith, was not dealing with this issue. My colleagues in the ministry were occasionally hearing similar stories and dealing with them as fanciful anecdotes. I suspected that was the very reason they were not hearing more of them: they were not taking them seriously.

Episodes in the Life of a House

In order for me to deal with these experiences, I had to accommodate them within my pattern of belief. The scriptures certainly made clear to me that there was a dual nature to reality: a physical world in which we lived, and moved, and had our existence, and a spiritual world that transcended time and space, and yet, was coexistent with and interpenetrating the physical world.

Once I had disposed of the notion that God dispensed with natural laws in the biblical period to accomplish the interaction with humans deemed necessary for redemption, I began to wonder why the experiences noted in the Bible were not still occurring in our time frame. Perhaps they were, but we were treating them in a different way—as fantasy. My perception was that modern psychology, until recently, would consider suspect those who heard voices and communicated with spiritual beings, or saw visions, or had revelations which spawned new religious thinking. This was the stuff of cults and quacks, and perhaps, even drug-induced hallucinations. And yet, people were having experiences that caused them to question the nature of reality, the nature of God, the meaning of eternal life, and the incursion of spiritual influences into our daily existence.

Seminary education did not prepare us adequately to deal with these questions. We were well prepared as preachers, educators, counselors, biblical scholars, theologians, historians, and church administrators. We were well versed in the church's need to address the issues of the day and to follow the agenda that society was listing for the church. But somehow, we didn't learn much about the priestly function of the ministry; it is not the administration of the sacraments, but the role of spiritual leader and guide.

In virtually every culture there are men and women who are experienced in making the connection between the physical and spiritual worlds. They have been known to us as "medicine men," shamans, *staretz*, mystics, priests, and by many other names. The Romans referred to their high priest as "pontifex maximus," literally "bridge maker," one who can transcend the gap between the world of humans and the world of the gods. In Celtic tradition, the Druids had shamans who were known as "walkers between worlds," who could move through the "thin places" and encounter the world of the spirit.

In Christianity, Jesus is represented as the great Mediator between God and God's creatures, the one who opens "the way" and becomes "the door," by which we can enter the spiritual realm. According to the gospels and the writings of Paul, Jesus demonstrated his ability to mediate between the two

The Mysticism of Ordinary and Extraordinary Experience

realms of existence, and perhaps, help us to understand that they are not as separate as we might tend to think they are. Heaven is the spiritual world that is around us and within us, and it is possible for us to become aware of its existence.

As pastor and priest, I have learned to be sensitive to the questions people ask about certain experiences which they do not understand. People do indeed have unusual experiences that seem to transcend what we have come to accept as the physical world. There are many that I have talked with who have stated that they have been unwilling to discuss these experiences with their fellow Christians and church members—and often with their pastors—because of a fear of ridicule and rejection. As ministers, we need to listen with greater sensitivity to these accounts, and to help persons interpret their meaning in the context of the Christian faith.

The experiences that have become a part of my own research are often difficult to label. Indeed, various theologians, psychologists, and researchers have established their own criteria for what constitutes a "mystical" experience. There is even an overlapping of criteria for mystical and "paranormal" experiences. In the studies that I have done I have used the broadest criteria for defining the experiences, and for the most part, permitted the respondents to describe what they consider unusual events that have some impact upon their religious faith or raise questions which they would consider religious in nature.

"Mystical experiences" are those experiences which enable the person to have a direct awareness of a spiritual reality or a realm of existence beyond the one which the person normally occupies. Although mystical experiences often defy rational attempts to explain either their appearance or their cause, they do not have to be irrational. A common experience in the life of a Christian, such as receiving the sacrament of Holy Communion, may trigger an awareness of the spiritual.

Paranormal experiences are those events that are perceived by the person to run counter to what is commonly considered "natural law." The issue of whether these events are quantifiable physical phenomena or the product of the percipient's mind is not in question. If a person believes an event to have occurred and that belief has an effect upon a person's faith, behavior, or worldview, then it is worthy of consideration.

Paranormal experiences include, but are not limited to, psychokinesis (movement without physical cause), extrasensory perception, precognition (knowing of an event before it occurs), clairvoyance and clairaudience (visual or auditory perception of current events or people without ordinary means of knowing), perception of apparitions, and out-of-body experiences.

Not all paranormal experiences are mystical in nature. They do not necessarily bring one to an awareness of the presence of God, or of a spiritual being, or even possess what may be termed a "religious" context. In other words, some people claim to have experienced paranormal events which they say have had no effect upon their religious faith or personal philosophy. However, because paranormal experiences very often open the door to the possibility of mystical experiences, and in many cases have preceded a mystical event, they should not be dismissed out of hand.

The phenomenon of the "haunted house" is all too common to be treated merely as a Halloween story. The realm of human experience transcends the sphere of earth. If we demand that our faith accepts it, perhaps we should permit our hearts and minds to entertain the possibility as well.

Spirits among Us

WHY DO GHOSTS HANG around the living? Don't they have anything better to do in the afterlife, whatever that is?

A group of spiritual seekers gathered in Stella's living room. I had been invited to share some insights from the perspective of the church and its tradition. I spoke about those incidents in the Bible where "ghosts" are mentioned, thus implying that ancient peoples believed in the existence of spirits, and that many cultures included some interaction with the dead as part of their superstition.

As I made my presentation to the group, I noticed a man sitting apart from the rest. Actually, he was in the next room, sitting in one of the dining room chairs. He was leaning forward, with his elbow on his knee and smoking a cigarette. At least he held the cigarette in his hand, because I couldn't see any smoke. He would occasionally put it to his lips as if taking a drag, but there was no glow to the cigarette.

Since no one else was in the dining room, the lights were off, and I could only see the man in the dim shadows. He seemed tall and thin, wearing a dress shirt, buttoned at the collar, but no tie. He was listening intently to what I had to say.

During the refreshment break I walked over to the dining room intending to invite the man to join the rest of the group, but he was gone. I thought he might be in the kitchen with the others, but he was nowhere to be found. I was puzzled by the strange man who chose to be alone and not participate with the others, nor introduce himself at the beginning of the session.

Stella was at the kitchen sink holding a paper cup filled with the fruit punch she had made. I asked her about the man in the dining room, describing his appearance and mannerism. Her eyes got bigger as she stared at me in disbelief, not noticing that the cup had slipped from her grasp.

Spirits among Us

When she recovered from her initial shock, she asked me for more details about the man.

Finally, she said, "That was my husband. He died last year of lung cancer. He always sat in that chair smoking a cigarette before dinner, his elbow on his knee just as you described. I had always felt his presence in this house. Sometimes I thought I saw a moving shadow and looked more closely—but nothing."

I had no explanation to offer, just conjecture. I had read much of the literature on the subject and even had experienced paranormal events in the house in Martins Creek, but this was the first time that something that wasn't there had stimulated my sense of sight.

Stella was now excited, spreading the news to her guests of this "sighting." You didn't have to convince them—that was the reason they had gathered in this place. Most of them, at one time or another, had had similar experiences. Now they were looking for explanations.

Based on my own inquiries into the subject, I proceeded to tell them that I thought there might be several possibilities, including the hypothesis that the essence of a person is somehow infused into the environment with which the person was most associated or where something traumatic had occurred, such as his or her death. Those with special gifts might be able to discern that spiritual essence and elicit information about the departed. I knew that there were a few in the group who practiced "psychometry" whereby they would hold an object most closely connected with the departed, either to establish a link to that person's spirit or to draw from the object itself the meaningful aspects of the person's life.

Among the ancient Celtic peoples there was a belief that the natural world was inhabited by spirits who took up residence in rocks and trees, streams and fields. The Greeks had their nymphs—the dryads who presided over forests and trees, the naiads who inhabited brooks, streams, and fountains—but these were divinities, divine essences that were a form of panentheism, literally "God in all." The Druids, Celtic shamans, were very adept at eliciting wisdom from the natural world and recognized that certain objects could be associated with persons who had lived in the area centuries earlier. By touching the object, they could discern its history and recall the ancient secrets.

In Stella's house, it was not a particular object, but the entire residence, that seemed infused with her husband's spirit. The primary reasons for the spirits of the dead to return was a sense of unfulfilled business that they wanted to accomplish, perhaps the communication of something they felt was important to them or to the ones they loved. Others might have experienced a violent or sudden death so that their consciousness had no time to adjust to a transition from the physical to spiritual existence. A third and most common manifestation is to assure loved ones that they were fine or to check on family and friends to see that they were doing well.

A member of my congregation, whom I had interviewed for my doctoral project in mysticism, reported that while she was pregnant her mother had died. After the birth of her granddaughter the woman appeared in the bedroom, looked down at the crib, smiled, and was gone.

I asked her if she thought that this might be a projection on her part of her need to have her mother's approval and that she had hallucinated the appearance to meet her own psychological needs. She said that she thought her mother's manifestation was not for the sake of her daughter, but for her own satisfaction and to express her approval and love.

Ghosts are so much a part of our culture and the religions of the world that they are either an inherent part of the human ego-defense system that denies the possibility of one's own non-existence or they are indeed a non-provable reality. While I have had much interest in this phenomenon, I never wanted to spend my entire life communicating with the spiritual realm to the exclusion of life in the present moment. My prayer life has assured me that the divine is present in the world I can see with my physical senses. It is enough to practice the presence of God in this world. While I welcomed any insight these discarnate spirits cared to give, that knowledge had to be tempered with my own perception of reality. I have always mistrusted people like Jerry Falwell or Pat Robertson who claimed that God was speaking to them. When God speaks to me, God usually says something altogether different. One must be careful in discernment. Sometimes, the spirits of those who have made the transition from this life don't know any more than they did while they were here. Why should we listen to them unless their message is consistent with scripture and tradition? And even that is subject to interpretation. What it comes down to is faith in the guidance of the Holy Spirit and the collective wisdom of all the saints.

I have an extensive library of thousands of books, most of which I haven't read. But I have good intentions. I have left instructions not to dispose of the library immediately, but to allow me some time to return in spirit to read them. Of course, this is foolishness since I believe I will have access to far greater knowledge than is contained in all my books. And besides, they will no longer be relevant to my future existence.

Seance in the Sanctuary

CHURCHES CAN BE VERY spooky places, especially at night. It is said that the spirits of the dead congregate in churches because they remember that while they inhabited this life the church was the place where they could find spiritual guidance and comfort for their soul. Perhaps they still gather in churches as an unseen cloud of witnesses listening to the Sunday sermon.

Or perhaps we are more sensitive to spiritual entities because of our own memories and associations. The dead were often buried in and around holy places, not only to be close to that which nurtured in them a belief in an afterlife, but that they would be remembered by their descendants. The sightings of ghosts in churches are historically quite common.

When I first came to Zion Church in the Pennsylvania German village of Womelsdorf, I was quite impressed with the beauty of this English Gothic "pocket cathedral." The open wooden beams, the intricate stone work, the marble railings, altar, and floor, and the beautiful stained-glass windows indicated that an earlier generation took their faith seriously and spared no expense in making their house of worship the finest possible.

Several features of the sanctuary and its furnishings hinted at the high liturgical tradition with which its congregation was familiar: the altar was high and exalted in front of a stone reredos on which two tall candles sat next to a pair of three smaller candles. In the chancel were two seven-branched candelabra on either side. High above the altar were two angels couchant holding a shield bearing the monogram of Christ and above them was a red sanctuary lamp, the *ner tamid* representing the eternal presence of God. A processional cross stood to the side in front of the organ. This indeed was a church worthy of a bishop. But even in the Mercersburg tradition of the Reformed Church, from which this congregation descended, that was going a bit too far.

The Mysticism of Ordinary and Extraordinary Experience

Illuminated only by the dimly lit sanctuary lamp, this would have been a scary place at night. Several years before my pastorate, my predecessor did have a frightening experience that nearly scared him out of his skin. Since the parsonage was attached to the rear of the church and shared a common wall, it was easy to use the church as a short-cut to the post office which was located opposite the front entrance. Late one night, not bothering to turn on the light, Clarence went from his office into the church and was halfway down the aisle when in the dim light he thought he saw something move in front of him. Moving a bit more hurriedly toward the front door, he then heard a low moan. When he got to the last row, a shadowy figure sat up in the pew. Clarence let out a scream; the entity in the pew screamed, and they both screamed together. Clarence made his way to the light switches and threw them on.

He was confronted by a homeless person who had found his way into the unlocked church and fell asleep. From that time on, Zion Church always kept its front door locked.

My family had had enough of ghostly experiences in our previous residence, and we had no desire to meet any more denizens of the other world. Unfortunately, we don't always have control over who we meet and who comes to us for help. Zion Church would have its own spectral residents.

My daughter Tasha's earliest memories in the parsonage were that of confronting a tall, dark-complected man in the cellar. Later she would also describe him as an Indian with feathers in his hair. We dismissed this as a childish fantasy common to many children, like the imaginary playmate. Yet this was no playmate, though his presence was non-threatening. Nevertheless, he sounded frightening. Tasha would not go to the cellar, and we did not encourage her.

Earl Ibach, a local historian and a member of the church Consistory, told us that there had been an Indian settlement in town. After all, this is where Conrad Weiser had lived. Weiser had been a friend of George Washington and helped negotiate treaties with the indigenous peoples. They valued his friendship and were his neighbors. It was Weiser's son-in-law, John Womelsdorf, who established a settlement and for whom the town had been named. Earl has written an extensive history of the area which was called "Tulpehocken," or "the land of the turtle." He said there might even have been an Indian cemetery located on the site of the church. It was not much of an explanation for Tasha's visitor unless one believed in ghosts.

Seance in the Sanctuary

Mary Ann became church secretary. The church office was just opposite the door to the parsonage, so it was very convenient. I often used the church office since it was larger than my own study. It wasn't long before Mary Ann began asking me to do much of my work in the church while she was typing. Whenever she sat at the typewriter she felt as though someone was standing behind her. It was the creepiest of sensations, she said. If she could not "see" whatever was there, did she have any sense about it, I asked her. She said it felt like it was an Egyptian man.

With my wife and daughter both describing a "man who isn't there," one perhaps a Native American, the other an Egyptian, that uneasy feeling began to return. It seemed we could not get away from mysterious occurrences, first in Martins Creek and now in Womelsdorf. Was it merely a coincidence, or was there some psychological abnormality that made my wife, daughter, and I predisposed to sensing what should not be present?

We certainly did not want to move again. We liked this town, this church, and these people. And in spite of its obvious drawbacks, we didn't mind living in an attached parsonage. I never had to worry about getting to church in a snowstorm. We did have to worry about the children making too much noise whenever something was going on next door. But the children thought it was great having the huge Sunday School room available. They could launch their airplanes from the balcony, play hide and seek among the many nooks and crannies, and invite their friends over for birthday parties.

Sometimes living next door was not a good idea, especially when it came to animals. I am in the habit of writing my sermons on a Saturday night. I maintain that I do it so that my thoughts will be fresh and up to minute. I have on occasion gone into the pulpit with the Sunday morning paper in hand as Karl Barth had suggested. Mary Ann says it is because I procrastinate. Though she didn't like typing my sermons in the middle of the night, she was often in the church office at 4:30 or 5:00 on a Sunday morning.

It was during Advent one year when I had finished my sermon relatively early, about 2:00 a.m. Mary Ann was typing away in the office while my brother-in-law, Bill, and I were sitting at the kitchen table talking. Bill was finishing up his third or fourth scotch and was feeling rather mellow when we heard a piercing cry from the church office. Two bats had gotten into the church and one of them had visited Mary Ann. Bill and I each grabbed a broom and headed for the church. We chased those flying mammals from one end of the building to the other. We hung over balconies,

The Mysticism of Ordinary and Extraordinary Experience

shot paperclips at the ceiling, and even sicced our barking beagle on them. Bill was so comical, glass of scotch in one hand, broom in the other, flailing away at the bats in their kamikaze-like runs. Finally, we got them to leave through a side door. The congregation was none the wiser, but several wondered why my family kept scanning the ceiling throughout the service.

Bats weren't the only creatures to visit Zion Church. Our cat loved to get into the organ chamber whenever someone would be foolish enough to leave the doors open. If a parishioner should be passing the church at an odd hour and heard the organ playing, perhaps I should say "sounding," it was because we were trying to scare the cat out of the pipes.

It was Underdog, our beagle, that almost caused cardiac arrest in one of the women working in the kitchen. The church kitchen is below ground level, with a number of casement windows providing ventilation. Underdog was the friendliest of beasts and would always go to the sound of the human voice. Unfortunately for Linda Gates it was her voice that attracted Underdog's curiosity and he poked his snout into the window just as Linda was looking up from the dishes. I was across the street in the parking lot when I heard her scream. Underdog was cowering in fear at our door. From that day on the kitchen windows were kept closed.

While we could laugh about the antics of our animals and the many incidents that form the precious memories of any family with young children, the unexplainable phenomena would recur. Mary Ann would be practicing the organ in the church while I would keep her company. On one occasion, I had left to make a phone call without telling her, but Mary Ann continued to talk to the person who was sitting in the shadows in the back of the nave. When I returned through the door next to her, she looked up incredulously and then stared into the darkness of the empty nave. There was no one there.

Craig had been the youth director of the church. He had committed suicide a few years earlier, but the rocking chair he had donated to the church office continued to be a permanent fixture, useful in creating the atmosphere I desired for counseling situations. He often sat in that chair while we talked about his continuing struggle with depression. It wasn't long after his death that from time to time we would notice the chair rocking of its own accord. Initially fearful, I began to accept this and would sometimes talk to Craig as if he were actually in the room. Perhaps he was.

When it was very quiet in the church, as it often was, one could stand at the top of the steps leading down to the Fellowship Hall and hear the faint echo of voices, the distant chattering of people perhaps gathered for a meeting. It was comforting to think that the saints of this church might still gather here to discuss the well-being of the congregation. Stephen Rose Benet once described the ghost of Daniel Webster appearing from time to time to ask, "How stands the Union?" I could imagine our spiritual ancestors still concerned for the faith of their heirs.

I had described to some non-church friends the eerie feelings that my wife and daughter were having at various times in the church and parsonage. One of our friends was a member of a group of people who gathered regularly to discuss their spiritual journeys, to meditate and to pray together, and to hold healing circles for those in need. She suggested that the group might meet at our place. Perhaps some of the more sensitive persons within the group might have the same feelings and be able to lend some guidance.

The leader of the group was a retired postal worker named George Ulle. Several years earlier, George had drifted off to sleep on his sofa while watching a baseball game. During that time, he said that he felt himself leave his body and go to where his wife, June, had been working as a nurse in the Reading Hospital. When June returned home, George was able to relate in detail all that occurred to her during the time that he was asleep. He became aware that something unusual was happening.

During one of his subsequent out-of-body excursions June heard a voice coming from George's body that sounded like George, but wasn't. The voice had a strong German accent and used many German words. George said that he was unfamiliar with the German language.

What he did tell us was that during his trance-like state a young German woman named Katie was speaking through him. He described Katie as a fun-loving girl who had been killed in a skiing accident when she crashed into an automobile. Her name had been Katrinka Knockstead from Regensburg. Katie had been coming to him and through him for several years to provide spiritual guidance and answer questions that those in the group might have. George would have no knowledge of what Katie was saying through him unless June recorded each of the sessions. I noticed that several members of the group also had their own tape recorders. (During the time that I had attended the sessions of this group I also had made many recordings.)

George suggested that I might want a private interview with Katie. While the group continued their own prayers and discussion in our living

The Mysticism of Ordinary and Extraordinary Experience

room, Mary Ann and I went with George into the church. He lay down on the floor in the middle of the transept and proceeded to enter a trance state. We noticed a slight stiffening of his body and then the thumb of his right hand began to make a circular motion against his leg. June told us that this was a sign that Katie was now present in George's body.

Katie spoke to us in terms that communicated a profound kindness and love. She said nothing that contradicted my beliefs, except for the very fact I was listening to a man lying on the floor of my church saying that he was someone else. It was most bizarre, but not at all frightening. I did not know what to make of this, nor did it enter my mind that some people might disapprove of what was happening. I was going to listen to Katie and then evaluate what she said based on its own merits. For all I knew, I could have been listening to an aspect of George's persona or, for that matter, a very elaborate charade. I intended to approach this as a researcher with an open but slightly skeptical mind.

Those within the group never used the word "séance" since it conjured up images of people sitting around in a circle trying to talk with the dead. And yet, this is what we were doing. Katie said that her colleagues in the spiritual realm often took offence that we would consider them "dead." "We are very much alive," she would say, "just not in a physical body."

What was most unbelievable about this event is that we were believing it. We were talking with Katie as though she was some traveler just returned from a far country and was relating the wonders and mysteries of an exotic land. I kept saying to myself, "Is this for real? Is this 'Katie' merely an aspect of George's persona or, for that matter, an elaborate charade? I'll sort this out later. Let me just get the information now and we will have time to analyze afterwards." It sounded something like I have often told members of my congregation when confronted with sudden tragedy: "Now is the time to walk by faith and not by sight. Trust God and meaning will come in due time." If this is where God was leading me at the present time, then who am I to resist. If it is not of God, then I must trust God to lead me in the right path.

In describing the nature of the spiritual realm, Katie said that there were many souls who were confused and lost and looking for guidance. They were seeking the Christ, the Light of God, but for one reason or another were either disoriented or resisting help. Yes, there were some who were very negative and even demonic. It would not be hard to recognize these entities should they appear. "For this reason," she said, "you must always ask for the protection of Christ and surround yourself with his light and love. You know what the Bible says about discerning the spirits."

When a person becomes spiritually aware or is perceived by these entities as being able to recognize their existence and presence, they will do all they can to attract attention. "When you were in Martins Creek," Katie explained, "you lived in a house close to the cemetery and the church. These are two places where many spirits congregate because it is often the site of their last contact with their earthly life. Because you are a minister, they believe that you were able to help them. They did not intend to harm you by what they did; they only wanted to let you know that they were there. There are many in this church who come to hear you. When you preach on Sunday morning, do you think you are only preaching to those whom you can see? There are others where I am who also want to hear about the Christ. When you hear sounds or see something which you cannot explain, do not be afraid. These are only signs that they are here and want your help. Show them the way to Christ and they will go."

Our discussion in the sanctuary lasted about forty-five minutes. For the next ten years, I attended many other sessions with Katie, taking extensive notes and making recordings. Eventually we seemed to move beyond where the group was going as new spiritual explorers took our place. I have always maintained an interest in the spiritual world and in mystical encounters, but unlike many within George's group I cannot devote my life to living in the psychic world. While it is absolutely essential that I assist others in their spiritual journeys and encourage other clergy to listen to the stories of their parishioners, I cannot invest all my time exploring the spiritual frontiers of another world. One must live in the moment of existence that is now and deal with the issues that are at hand. The spiritual impinges upon the physical in so many ways that it is not necessary to go to extremes to encounter it. Simply be aware of the spiritual world and it will be enough.

Unexpected Visitors

DO GHOSTS HAVE CALENDARS? Do they keep appointments on PCs and iPhones? Is there some cosmic secretary to tell them when they should make an appearance?

It seems that there are certain dates and seasons on our calendar when either the veil is lifted just a bit or becomes a little more transparent—the so-called "thin" places or times when another reality impinges upon our physical existence. Whether it's the Witches Sabbath of Walpurgisnacht on the eve of Beltane or the gathering of all spiritual beings on the eve of All Hallows' or Samhain, there are those times when we have a better opportunity to socialize with those who have departed the mortal life.

I have often wondered how they know when to show up. Or do ghosts just hang around waiting for us to acknowledge their presence? Aside from Samhain or Halloween, the most haunted time of year seems to be around the winter solstice or yuletide. At Newgrange in Ireland, there is an aperture, *Brugh na Boinne*, in the great megalithic enclosure so that on the shortest day of the year at dawn, a thin finger of light enters the dark recesses of the inner chamber. This is the great divide between the worlds of darkness and light. It is the thin place where the entities of another world come together to illumine one's own destiny.

Perhaps, it is we who draw the veil and uncover our own darkness, guided by the ghosts of memory who come to impart lost wisdom, or comfort in times of painful separation, or the reassurance that nothing is ever lost but continues in another dimension.

In December 1843, Charles Dickens published *A Christmas Carol*, certainly one of the greatest ghost stories ever written. The three specters that appear to Ebenezer Scrooge on Christmas Eve come to remind him of what he has missed in life as the years passed, of his current responsibility to fulfill the purpose of his living, and of his ultimate destiny that one can also be dead after dying.

I do not believe that ghosts appear for our entertainment or handouts of candy, but to remind us of who we are and of what we are a part of. The nature of apparitional consciousness may have its own purpose and function, but often it is out of our own need that they become apparent to us. There has always been a question as to whether ghosts are objective or subjective. Do they exist independent of the observer, or are they "daggers of the mind," created by our own psychological needs or induced by some collective hallucination or cultural influence?

We must continue to explore the nature of alternative realities, of the existence of ghosts and the evidence for post-mortem survival, believing as Hamlet did that there are worlds of thought and information beyond our comprehension.

I tend to be very busy during the Christmas season, so my advice to any ghosts who have a desire to communicate with me—please call ahead for an appointment.

Originally written for *The Searchlight*, Academy of Spirituality and Paranormal Studies, Inc. Volume 20.4 (December 2011).

Deathbed Visions and Near-Death Experiences

IS POST-MORTEM SURVIVAL "TESTABLE?" No, it is not subject to empirical study. The scientific view is that the universe is material and that mind is a by-product of the brain. When the brain dies, its conscious abilities end.

However, theology says that mind or Spirit existed before matter and that matter was created by the thought of God. Dawson Church, in his book, *Mind to Matter*, makes the case that the mind creates matter, that the brain produces an energy field whereby thoughts can become things. Church draws from hundreds of studies to demonstrate that there is a universal mind accessed by the individual mind that can produce change and create matter. While a scientific perspective is helpful in the study of near-death experiences and deathbed visions, we need to recognize that science is a closed box designed to investigate the material universe and is only recently exploring the quantum field of creative energy. There are scientists who believe that paranormal events have occurred but cannot explain them, while others still consider them as pure hokum.

There are several areas of research and evidence that suggest life after death. Ghosts, reincarnation, premonitions relating to impending death, apparitions at the time of death, and afterdeath communication and signs. (I refer you to *Messages: Signs, Visits, and Premonitions from Loved Ones Lost on 9/11* by Bonnie McEneaney.) In this chapter, I would like to consider deathbed visions and near-death experiences.

My own background in this field stems from an interest in the Christian mystical tradition and manifestations of the paranormal in my own experiences. My doctoral dissertation was on "Mysticism and Ministry" in which I interviewed Berks County, Pennsylvania, residents, members of the United Church of Christ, who said that they had had experiences which they regarded as mystical. One of my mentors was Dr. Karlis Osis who wrote the book, *What They Saw at the Hour of Death*, about his research on over a thousand cases of deathbed visions by doctors and nurses. Dr. Osis helped me design my research project. I have also had conversations with Dr. Raymond Moody who pioneered the study of near-death experiences and wrote *Life After Life*, and also Dr. Kenneth Ring author of *Life at Death*. All three were speakers at conferences of the Academy of Spirituality and Paranormal Studies of which I was president. However, I do want to make it clear that while I have investigated the subject, I am not a scientist or medical expert. My point is that near-death experiences and deathbed visions have been reported with such frequency that they warrant continued research. We will leave it to science to explain the "how" and to theology and faith to address the "why."

Evidence and Proof

There is a difference between proof and evidence. Evidence is the accumulation of data which leads one toward a particular conclusion. Proof is based on scientific "cause and effect" inductive reasoning that is based on observation and inference. Scientific proof demands that the experience can be predictable and replicated. Since we cannot deliberately kill someone in the lab and hope that you don't succeed so he can come back and tell you of his experience, it's not replicable. But you can collect stories, and the preponderance of this material suggests the conclusion.

Paranormal experiences are those which are alongside the normal, but beyond scientific proof. These are the events of mystical experience that are more apprehended by faith rather than sensory input. Some would say that they are events that bypass the senses or, in other words, extra-sensory, as in ESP. We accept the resurrection of Jesus on the basis of faith, not fact.

Near-Death Experiences

Raymond Moody examined thousands of cases in a cross-cultural study and found a similar progression of experiences in those who were clinically dead but were resuscitated. Many physicians say that this is a fallacious term since the definition of death is that you don't return from it. The experience consists of hearing a humming sound, total darkness, perception of a tunnel through which one moves, encountering a being of light who confronts you with your own life experience as a gestalt, helps you evaluate it, and then tells you to return because it's not your time.

The Mysticism of Ordinary and Extraordinary Experience

Some physicians say that this is purely psychological, the brain resisting the concept of death. The mind is a product of the brain. The cerebral cortex is where cognition takes place: your awareness of who and where you are and all your thought processes. Without that, you cannot know anything, you cannot experience anything, and you cannot sense anything, so when the brain ceases to function, you are dead. The only consolation is that when you are dead you don't know it. So, if the scientists are right there is nothing to worry about. Woody Allen said, "I'm not afraid of dying; I just don't want to be there when it happens."

However, there are some cases that contradict this. Pam Reynolds, a singer from Atlanta, had an NDE (near-death experience) during a brain operation to remove an aneurysm. While on the table she flat lined—no brain activity, no blood flowing in her brain. She was clinically dead, but she was able to make several observations about the procedure which were later confirmed by medical personnel as very accurate. While fully anesthetized, with sound-emitting earplugs to check the function of the brain stem to ensure that her brain was non-responsive, Pam's ordeal began. Dr. Robert F. Spetzler, the surgeon from the Barrow Institute at Phoenix, Arizona, was sawing into her skull when Pam suddenly heard the saw and began to observe the surgical procedure from a vantage point over his shoulder. She also heard what the nurses said to the doctors. Upon returning to consciousness, she was able to accurately describe the unique surgical instrument used and report the statements made by the nurses.

Kenneth Ring, at the University of Connecticut, and other researchers, corroborated Moody's findings and speculate about the possibility of the mind existing beyond the brain. Near-death experiences give some indication of that.

The elements described in Moody's research are:

1. Hearing sounds such as buzzing.
2. A feeling of peace and painlessness.
3. Having an out-of-body experience.
4. A feeling of traveling through a tunnel.
5. A feeling of rising into the heavens.
6. Seeing people, often dead relatives.
7. Meeting a spiritual being such as God.
8. Seeing a review of one's life.

9. Feeling a reluctance to return to life.[1]

Seeing dead relatives at the time of actual death or during the near-death experience while in a coma is fairly frequent. The world-renowned cardiologist Pim van Lommel reported this example in the words of a patient:

> During my NDE following a cardiac arrest, I saw both my dead grandmother and a man who looked at me lovingly but whom I didn't know. Over ten years later my mother confided on her deathbed that I'd been born from an extramarital affair; my biological father was a Jewish man who'd been deported and killed in World War II. My mother showed me a photograph. The unfamiliar man I'd seen more than ten years earlier during my NDE turned out to be my biological father.[2]

It has often been reported that just before death persons will see their lives pass before them. It is not a linear progression but rather as a totality, a flash, a gestalt, without regard to time or space. During this life review the person experiences all that has been done and thought during one's life, like the dumping of a super computer's memory cache. This is done in the presence of another entity, often called a "being of light," who helps the person evaluate his or her past.

Instantaneously, they are where they concentrate upon (*non-locality*), and they can talk for hours about the content of the life review even though the resuscitation only took minutes. Lommel shares this statement from one who experienced a NDE:

> All of my life up till the present seemed to be placed before me in a kind of panoramic, three-dimensional review, and each event seemed to be accompanied by a consciousness of good or evil or with an insight into cause or effect. Not only did I perceive everything from my own viewpoint, but I also knew the thoughts of everyone involved in the event, as if I had their thoughts within me. This meant that I perceived not only what I had done or thought, but even in what way it had influenced others, as if I saw things with all-seeing eyes. And so even your thoughts are apparently not wiped out. And all the time during the review the importance of love was emphasised. Looking back, I cannot say how long this life review and life insight lasted, it may have been long, for every subject came up, but at the same time it seemed just a fraction of

---

1. Moody, *Life After Life*, 26–62.
2. Lommel, *Consciousness Beyond Life*, 32–33.

a second, because I perceived it all at the same moment. Time and distance seemed not to exist. I was in all places at the same time, and sometimes my attention was drawn to something, and then I would be present there.[3]

Scientific Hypotheses

Carl Sagan, in the last chapter called "The Amniotic Universe" in his book *Broca's Brain*,[4] refers to the studies conducted by the physician-psychiatrist, Stanislav Grof. Grof posits that the near-death experience may be a replay of the birth experience. The latent memory of being born is embedded in the brain. The tunnel being the birth canal; the sensation of floating in the air would evoke the sensation of floating in amniotic acid during gestation; the bright light being the delivery room; the voices are the doctors and nurses. Ken Ring says that while this may be analogous, it is too simplistic.

Several theories on the origin of NDEs have been proposed. Some think the experience is caused by physiological changes in the brain as cells die as a result of cerebral anoxia and possibly also caused by the release of endorphins. Other theories relate to psychological reactions to approaching death. But there has been no scientifically definitive study to explain the cause and content of an NDE.

Deathbed Visions

Deathbed visions throughout history are not unusual. The experience of dying has been observed and recorded by countless physicians and nurses, hospice workers, and clergy, and of course relatives.

The English poet, William Blake, witnessing the death of his brother, Robert, remarked that he saw his brother's soul as a coalescence of light over his body which moved toward an open window and "ascend heavenward, clapping its hands for joy."

For centuries, many have believed that souls matter and are substantial. Ancient Egyptians buried their dead in tombs called *"het-ka,"* or house of the *ka*. The *ka* is the essential spirit of the person. Another component of the postmortem existence was the *ba*, or soul, depicted as a bird with a

3. Lommel, *Consciousness Beyond Life*, 36.
4. Sagan, *Broca's Brain*, 301–7.

human head, which was free to roam around. Tombs were furnished with doors so that the *ba* could circulate until it united with its *ka*, or personality and intelligence. Food and drink were also supplied to sustain the *ba*.

The early Pennsylvania Germans, carrying their old world traditions, often built into a room of their eighteenth century homes, a "*seelen fenster*," or "soul window." In this room the elderly family members, or those believed to be terminally ill, slept, and upon death the deceased person's soul escaped to the outside through the soul window. (These soul holes were also used as rifle holes to send the souls of their attackers to God.) In some hospitals, nurses still open windows when a person dies. Hopi Indians would also orient a dying person toward an opening.

Ancient Celtic peoples believed in "thin places" and "thin times" when the divide between the physical and spiritual worlds became transparent and there was interaction between the one who is about to cross over and those who had already done so. Whether or not these universal beliefs determine what the dying say they see, or whether they confirm a reality remains to be seen.

Karlis Osis and Erlandur Haraldson did a study in the United States and in Iceland in which they interviewed doctors and nurses in well over a thousand cases in which dying persons reported what they saw at the time of their death. Out of 35,540 observable cases, 1,310 of the patients saw apparitions and 884 had visions. In most cases there was a greeting from those who had predeceased the patients, a life review, assurance of comfort and well-being, and the presence of religious figures or angels. In some cases, the presence of apparitions or feelings of presence are perceived by others in the room.

Ethan Allen, the Revolutionary War general and victor at Ticonderoga was on his deathbed. His doctor told him: "the angels are waiting for you," and he said, "Waiting, are they? Waiting, are they? Well, damn them, let 'em wait." I think in most cases, the patient is comforted by those who are waiting for him.

Let me cite a few cases that I witnessed:

W. Ray Klopp at the time of his death in Myerstown was introducing me to persons who were present in the room whom I did not see. "There were angels here." He felt very comforted by this. His last act was to raise his arms as though he was going with them. (Incidentally, the up-raised arms are the Egyptian hieroglyphic for the *ka*.) This gesture is quite common. My grandmother did this just before she died.

The Mysticism of Ordinary and Extraordinary Experience

Both Marvin's and Katie's encounters with deceased relatives just prior to their own deaths raised similar questions about the paranormal, dual realities, and one's subconscious bringing comfort as the body deteriorates.

Karl Pribram's holonomic brain is said to store all our memories, and perhaps at death the release of endorphins triggers the stored memories to provide comfort. Or are we surrounded by the unseen cloud of witnesses who become apparent in times of crisis?

A nurse at Reading Hospital sensed the presence of a fifteen-year-old accident victim hovering above her body as the physicians were working on her. I could hear her saying, "Why can't they do something? Can't they do anything?" She died. Leo Frangipane, a surgeon, told me that he remembered that case, or one similar, where a light seemed to envelop the body.

One person said they had met a Christ figure, but dressed as Detective Columbo in a trench coat. Another person who had converted from Islam to Christianity saw Jesus and Mohammad arguing about who would get him. In some ways, the deathbed vision is like a dream in which our encrypted memories play-act to bring about resolution.

For many of us, our most precious memories are those of sitting down to dinner with family and friends. In the opening scene of the film, "Antwone Fisher," is a banquet where all the relatives who have passed on gather to welcome Antwone. It is no wonder that many religions have a meal as an integral part of their faith. The Messianic Banquet may also be a deep-seated psychological manifestation of welcome, comfort, reunion, and joy.

The Exorcist

ON SEVERAL OCCASIONS I have received calls from ministerial colleagues to tell me of unusual experiences that they have encountered in their ministries. Because of my research projects and lectures that I had given about mysticism and the paranormal, I had apparently earned a reputation as one familiar with strange encounters with the spiritual dimension.

While I preferred to deal with those experiences in which persons felt close to the divine or somehow sense the immanence of God, all too often I would hear stories that bordered on the demonic. Church members would tell their pastors of troubling experiences that were disturbing or even terrifying. Since the seventeenth century the Roman Catholic Church would have at least one priest in each diocese trained to deal with demonic possession. Since the revision of Vatican guidelines in 1999, a priest who uses a rite of exorcism can do so only after the alleged possessed person has been evaluated by medical personnel to be sure that he or she is not suffering from mental or physical problems, including addiction to or use of drugs.

I was getting a reputation for being a sort of regional exorcist who would be called upon when persons felt that they had been visited by residents of the ghostly world. There is a difference, however, between seeing an apparition and being possessed by another entity. While I am not a practicing psychologist, I have studied abnormal psychology and the psychology of consciousness. It is important, therefore, to ascertain whether the person interviewed has a psychological basis for the experience. Is there something in their physiology or something that is happening in their lives or something that has affected them to make them more susceptible to the perception of an alternate reality? In the demon-haunted universe of many of Shakespeare's characters, it is Macbeth who asks, "Is this a dagger which I see before me . . . or is this a false creation proceeding from the heat-oppressed brain" (2.1). Where do these images come from? If we start with the

The Mysticism of Ordinary and Extraordinary Experience

premise that the world is demon-filled and spirit-filled then we are going to operate on the assumption that these entities may be trying to make contact with persons who are mentally or physically susceptible to them. I've often gone to people as they were dying and sensed the presence of other persons around them, so the question is: is it something that is actually taking place in the mind of the beholder, or can others be witnesses to the event?

The pastor of a large congregation called me one morning and said that the daughter of one of his members believed that she had seen a strange man in the corner of her bedroom. She had told her father that she did not see the man directly, but only as a shadow. When the ten-year-old would try to focus on the space where he seemed to be, there was nothing there. She would only glimpse enough of him to know that he was there. The girl was so terrified that she could not sleep at night for that was when the unseen presence was strongest.

I visited the family and they told me of the several encounters that the child had related. I was aware that impressionable children sometimes experience imaginary playmates to fill psychological or social needs. They appear real to the child and interact in playful ways. These impressions can be very vivid, but do not seem to be alarming. Psychologists recognize this as a product of the child's mind to create that which he or she may need. I was thinking that this might be the case. But what this young girl saw or felt was no playmate.

Her father said that he had a video camera and went into his daughter's room and recorded a voice that he had not audibly heard in the room, but was on the soundtrack saying, "What are you doing here? Get out of here!" It was a male voice and seemed to come from the corner where the girl said that she sensed the presence. The father asked me, "What can we do about it?"

Not having a liturgy for exorcism, I asked that we form a prayer circle with him and some of his relatives and friends. We offered prayers for protection, surrounded the apartment with light, and commended the spirit or presence to the light of God. I had heard months later that the daughter and her family were no longer troubled by the presence of the unseen visitor.

Another ministerial colleague telephoned me to ask for some advice for one his families that had recently purchased a home in Leesport, Pennsylvania. I offered to meet with them at their home. Before I inquired about why they had called their pastor, we walked through the house. There was a feeling of foreboding in various parts of the house. I, too, was able to sense the uneasiness which they had experienced. They knew something was there, but they couldn't put their finger on it, so to speak. They were not aware of the history of the house, whether some traumatic event had occurred there in years past. There was no paranormal activity, just a shared feeling of dread, as though something unpleasant or evil was about to happen.

I offered to return the next morning, a Saturday, when the entire family could be present. I used a liturgy for the Blessing of a Home that came from a Greek Orthodox rite. Beginning with prayers around the kitchen table, we went from room to room, using separate prayers for each room. Since I was not a priest of the Eastern Rite, I did not use icons or holy water, although these were customarily used. Part of the prayers was for the casting out of any negative influences and to exorcize any evil spirits. After we moved through all the rooms of the house, we went outside and circled the house, with prayers at each side. And then the final prayers for each member of the family.

Was this ritual in and of itself efficacious? Perhaps. But what I believe was more helpful was the assurance in the minds of the residents that they were being protected by divine help. They were no longer fearful, and within a few weeks their house had become their home.

In a university town where I was pastor, we would often have international exchange students worship with us. Moses Awatona was from Kenya, probably in his fifties, and had been coming to our church throughout the semester. He was a deeply spiritual man and probably had children back in the old country. Moses was very faithful in his attendance and very proud of his country. Prior to a United Church of Christ World Ministries conference, I obtained an array of international flags to display from the canopy surrounding the nave. During our sharing of concerns Moses stood up and expressed how proud he was. He said, "That's my flag."

The next semester his brother, Patrick, came to the United States and the two students moved into an apartment in Reading. A short time later, a disastrous fire struck. They lost all of their possessions, and I believe that traumatized him severely. Church members came together to provide clothing and other items to get them back on their feet. Kutztown University students also came to their aid. But misfortune continued and Moses developed cirrhosis of the liver that would eventually prove fatal. He was hospitalized with a severe case of jaundice.

The disease was so severe that it affected his brain's ability to understand the nature of reality. He was going in and out of a conscious state. When I went to visit him at the hospital there were a number of students in the room when I came in; in fact, probably more than should have been there. But considering that Moses was terminal, we were given some latitude. I walked in wearing my clerics, and upon seeing me, Moses' eyes grew wide, and in his delirium immediately shouted, "The devil's here to get me." As he thrashed about on his bed, I put my hand to his forehead and offered a prayer in the name of Jesus. His fears subsided and he became calm again and was able to converse with me and his friends. The next day he died.

Some time later, one of his friends, who was also a member of my church, commented on the exorcism I had performed. I told him that I didn't think I was calling out any demons, but simply letting Moses know and feel that he was not alone, that he was surrounded by a larger community of faith, those who were there physically and the unseen cloud of witnesses from the heavenly realm, and that he was secure in the arms of his heavenly Father.

The New Testament is filled with stories of healing, mostly by Jesus. In fact, that is the most common of his miracles. In a pre-scientific age when knowledge of medicine was very primitive, people believed that illness was caused by demons, especially mental illness. It may very well have been the case when Jesus healed the many with a frenzied spirit. The Gerasene demoniac may have been suffering from a bi-polar disorder, a form of manic depression. Or he may have been schizophrenic, or may have had a multiple personality disorder. These are three distinctive mental illnesses which ancient peoples could construe as demon possession.

When Jesus' disciples claimed that there were fraudulent healers who were performing exorcisms in the name of Jesus, even though they weren't followers of Christ, Jesus told them to let these unauthorized practitioners alone. If they are doing good work, then that in itself is a blessing, and what God wants them to do. To put it into contemporary terms, you don't have to be a follower of Christ to do God's will. Even Buddhists and Taoists and Muslims perform works of righteousness and should be commended.

I was once interviewed by a seminary student who was doing her doctoral research on spiritual warfare and the practice of exorcism in the church today. Our conversation led to a discussion on the nature of evil and its personification in the person of the devil. While it is obvious that evil exists in the world, that which is contrary to God's intention for humanity, you cannot blame it on a mythical figure. When Flip Wilson used to say, "The devil made me do it," he was giving expression to the human desire to avoid taking responsibility for our own actions. The theodicean question of why a loving and all-powerful God permits evil to exist is very complicated and has been argued for centuries. I would agree with Martin Luther who wrote in his famous hymn, "A Mighty Fortress is Our God":

> And though this world, with devils filled,
> should threaten to undo us,
> we will not fear, for God hath willed
> his truth to triumph through us.
> The Prince of Darkness grim,
> we tremble not for him;
> his rage we can endure,
> for lo, his doom is sure;
> one little word shall fell him.

Knowing that evil is doomed and will not prevail into the next life enables us to endure all the tragedies of this life. God's truth will triumph through us. In the meantime, we, too, must perform the acts of exorcism as we contend against the demonic powers that exist in our world today.

Pope Francis performed acts of exorcism during his visit to the United States. We have seen him touching countless persons with words of blessing—whether they are sick and lame, the socially oppressed and disadvantaged, those imprisoned in jails or in their own minds, those denied equal justice and equal opportunity, the poor, the hungry, the outcast, the lonely, and the abandoned. When Francis touched each of these persons, he was in essence saying that they are connected to the whole human family and to God. We are made whole when we are part of the whole. The act of healing is not only a mending of the body, but a binding of the soul. As one of the prayers of the church affirms, "we are all bound together in this bundle of life."

As Jesus told his disciples, we are followers of the Christ when we do the will of God, regardless of what faith we choose to be identified with. In fact, the word "religion" itself, derives from the Latin word "*re-ligio*," or "tied together." We are all bound together and bound to a loving Creator God.

Pope Francis, in his address to the United States Congress, said, "Now is the time for courageous actions and strategies, aimed at implementing a "culture of care." That is a phrase that should be embedded in all our hearts and minds as we seek to cast off all that separates us from the family of God. "A culture of care" will exorcize the demons of this world when we realize that we are all precious in the eyes of God and are all in need of healing and mending.

Born Again . . . and Again . . . and Again

Two lovers interested in spiritualism vowed that if either died, the one remaining would try to contact the partner in the other world within a short period of time after their dying. Unfortunately, a few weeks later the young man died in a car accident. His faithful sweetheart tried to contact him in the spirit world thirty days later.

At the seance she called out, "John, this is Martha. Do you hear me? A ghostly voice answered her, "Yes, Martha, this is John. I can hear you."

Martha tearfully asked, "Oh John, what is it like where you are?" "It's beautiful. There are azure skies, a soft breeze, sunshine most of the time."

"What do you do all day?" asked Martha. "Well Martha, we get up before sunrise, eat some good breakfast, and there's nothing but sex until noon. After lunch we nap until two and then have more sex until about five. After dinner we go at it again until we fall asleep about 11 pm."

Martha was somewhat shocked. "Is that what heaven really is like?" "Heaven? I'm not in heaven, Martha. I've been reincarnated as a jack rabbit in Arizona."

That's an old joke that has been making the rounds, but it does raise an interesting question: Is there more to life than our present experience of it?

While we have generally been aware of the prominence of belief in reincarnation in Eastern religions, it has often been minimized and less understood in Western culture. Let's consider an overview of reincarnation in Western myth and story, an analysis of references in the three Middle Eastern religions, and the relevance of reincarnation to Christian faith and teaching.

Several years ago, some itinerant evangelists were making the rounds in our neighborhood, carrying their limp-bound Bibles and a handful of tracts to hand out. Usually, I don't have time to respond to them, but occasionally I just want to engage in dialogue and respond to their question "Are you saved?" When the young preacher asked me, "Are you born again," I told him, "Yes, many times," and proceeded with a discourse on reincarnation. That, he did not want to hear.

Most Christian mystics did not spend much time thinking about reincarnation. If we understand mysticism to be the awareness of the presence of God, of being one with God, of enjoying and spiritually growing in our relationship with God, then reincarnation needs to be considered. Reincarnation is generally assumed to be the process whereby the soul at the time of death enters or incarnates into a new body. Some beliefs hold that this is immediate, while others believe that there is a waiting period where souls enjoy God's presence and have their desires fulfilled—in other words, Heaven. Madame Blavatsky, founder of Theosophy refers to this as the "false bliss" of Devanchan. In Roman Catholic thought, this intermediate state is Purgatory where the souls of dead evaluate their lives and are purged of their sins or impediments before moving on to the next stage of existence.

In appreciating the presence of God, the mystic seeks to discern God's intention for our being. Can it be fulfilled in one lifetime, or must one keep coming back for remedial education in learning the reason for existence? If we are one with the nature of God, as Jesus suggested, and God is in us, then God is also growing and accumulating experiences through the infinite expressions of life in the universe.

When I read in the morning newspaper of the rape and murder of a college student or the death of a two-year old from coronavirus or the police killing of a burglary suspect, I question the intention of their lives. Has the purpose of their brief existence been for their own spiritual growth, or did they live in order for others to learn from their experiences? What meaning can the uncompleted, unfulfilled life have? Often, we don't live for ourselves but for the meaning we have in the lives of others. Of course, I am applying human reasoning to the universe which may be beyond the scope of our thinking. The "why" of existence is one of the great imponderables of philosophy.

Throughout the world, some seventy percent of humans believe in reincarnation in one form or another. A Pew Research survey in December 2017 reported that thirty-three percent of all U.S. adults believe in reincarnation. The number is slightly higher (thirty-six percent) among Catholics. It is a topic of more than passing interest and many volumes have been written on the subject—some theological and philosophical, some scientific, and some anecdotal. There have been novels and movies

The Mysticism of Ordinary and Extraordinary Experience

based on the theory, and it has made the round of television talk-shows and even TV series.[1]

Many poets have articulated positions supporting reincarnation. William Wordsworth, wrote in "Intimations on Immortality":

> Our birth is but a sleep and a forgetting:
> The Soul that rises with us, our life's Star,
> Hath had elsewhere its setting,
> And cometh from afar.

Many writers have sought to deconstruct that stanza to show that Wordsworth and others believed in the pre-existence of the soul, that the concept of reincarnation is firmly rooted in the human psyche, and that it is part of the process of the spirit's infinite existence.

Reincarnation is the belief that the essence of a person, usually defined as "soul," returns to the body of another living being after death, sometimes described as the "transmigration of souls" or metempsychosis.

In Eastern religions, such as Hinduism, it is believed that it is possible to return as an animal or insect if one's karma is bad. Or if it is exceptional, one can return as a brahmin. Karma is the accumulation of good or bad deeds during a lifetime which is judged between lifetimes. The succession of incarnations is *samsara*, and the idea is for the soul or atman to break the succession of *samsara* and merge with Brahman, the Ultimate Reality.

In some western cultures which maintain a belief in reincarnation, the soul is regarded as immortal, created by God or derived from God, and may return only in the form of another human, but definitely not a jack rabbit.

In ancient Egyptian theology, based upon the Book of the Dead, a person is composed of the *ka* or spiritual essence, and the *ba*, which formed his personality. At the time of death, the *ka* and the *ba* would separate from the body. The *ka* was required to return to the body, which was preserved through mummification and placed in tombs, which in Egyptian was called *het-ka*, or "house of the *ka*." The concept was that you needed a place for the *ka* to inhabit until such time as it would merge again with the *ba* and form the *akh*, which was the spirit form of the deceased or ghostly essence.

The idea of this Egyptian view of reincarnation perhaps influenced many subsequent superstitions and beliefs. For example, when a person sneezes you say "Gesundheit" or "God bless you." You say this because

---

1. Pew Research Center, "'New Age' beliefs."

Born Again . . . and Again . . . and Again

when you sneezed, you were allowing the soul to escape the body, and you want to protect the person by asking God to keep the soul within the body. You also wanted to make sure that when you were asleep, you did not sleep with your mouth open lest you end up being someone else. The souls of the deceased will look for other bodies to inhabit, according to this ancient Egyptian perspective. You were very careful of ghosts and made sure you didn't come in contact with them and avoided cemeteries lest wandering spirits take over your body.

The Hebrews believed that God breathed his *ruach* into flesh, the substance of the earth, and man became a living being. This *ruach*, which is the breath or spirit of God, the essence of God that creates the body. The merger of spirit and body can be found in Genesis, but later on it developed that there was a unification of spirit and body, that the spirit generated the body, and they were one. That was much different from the duality of the Egyptian concept, and later, of the Greek "psyche" and "soma." The Hebrews came to believe that when the body died, this spiritual essence or life force known as the *nephesh* went to Sheol, a place of non-existence, like a warehouse of used souls. The essence of the Hebrew concept is that we are our bodies; we do not inhabit our bodies. There are, however, exceptions to that thought and various interpretations of the meaning of *nephesh*.

During the period of the Exile, when the Jews were held in captivity in Babylon, they most likely became exposed to the teachings of Zoroaster, whose philosophy was then current. Zoroaster held to a philosophy of dualism in which humans are distinct from other animals in that they possess a soul. Anyone who wishes to return to the lower world (earth) and is a doer of good, shall, according to his knowledge and conversation and actions, receive either a high position in society and sufficient wealth until he meets with a reward suited to his deeds. Some teachings indicate that evil persons are condemned to the bodies of vegetables, and the extremely wicked to the form of rocks.

The Magi who made an appearance at Jesus' birth were probably reincarnationists like the Pharisees who were influenced by Persia during the post-Babylonian captivity. Josephus indicates that the Pharisees believed that all souls are incorruptible; but that the souls of good people at death are only removed into other bodies, but that the souls of evil persons are subject to eternal punishment. (*Jewish War*, 2.7)

In the post-exilic period during which much of the Talmud was written, some rabbinic writers, who were the spiritual ancestors of the medieval

The Mysticism of Ordinary and Extraordinary Experience

kabbalists, could be said to possess a belief in reincarnation, although this was not a principle teaching of the Tanakh, Mishnah, or Talmud. In kabbalistic thought, there is the belief that a soul that has been unable to fulfill its function during its lifetime is given another opportunity to do so in a *"dybbuk"* form. The *dybbuk* ("attachment") was a possessing spirit who escaped or was rejected by Gehenna and supposedly leaves the host body once it has accomplished its goal, sometimes after being helped.

During the Hellenistic period, the three centuries before Christ, the dualism of the separation of *psyche* and *soma* at death became prominent and Socrates, Plato, and Pythagoras reputedly remembered past lives.

Jesus of Nazareth grew up in a culture where reincarnation may have been considered by many as a possibility. Jesus did not teach reincarnation, but was aware of the doctrine and did not refute it as he did others. Some scholars believe that Jesus derived much of his teachings from the Essenes who formed a community at Qumran on the Dead Sea and were responsible for the Dead Sea scrolls. Josephus says that the Essenes believed in the immortality of the soul and that the soul would return to the body after death (*Jewish War*, 2.7). Others argue that Josephus was referring to a bodily resurrection in which the soul would reincarnate in its original body.

In the Gospels, there are some passages that may indicate that the belief in reincarnation was held by some. In Matthew 11:13–15, Jesus refers to John the Baptist as "Elijah who is to come," although he could have been speaking metaphorically. In Matthew 16:13, when Jesus asked his disciples, "Who do men say that I am?" the disciples replied, "Some say John the Baptist, but others Elijah, and still others Jeremiah or one of the prophets." There are other passages that may hint at reincarnation, but they would be a stretch. Clearly the Pharisees believed in reincarnation, while the opposite party, the Sadducees, did not.

In the Gospel according to John, which was heavily influenced by Gnosticism, when Jesus confronts a man born blind, the disciples asked whether it was a result of his sin or that of his parents. We may see in this question the possibility of karmic law, or as Paul said, "we reap what we sow" (Gal 6:7), although he may be looking forward and not to a previous existence. The idea of metempsychosis was probably not in the mind of Paul, nor of the Christians of his generation, since they maintained a belief in the imminent return of Jesus in a spiritual form.

When it became evident that Christ would not be returning anytime soon, Christians, particularly those who belonged to the Gnostic groups—Ebionites, Valentinians, Ophites—adopted the belief that the soul would return in another form so as to fulfill a karmic law. There was a group, known as the pre-existiani, that included such writers and scholars as Justin Martyr (100–165 AD), Clement of Alexandria (150–220 AD), and Origin (185–254 AD). They taught the pre-existence of the soul and believed that the soul would re-imbody after death.

Origin, in *Contra Celsum* (1, xxxii), asked: "Is it not rational that souls should be introduced into bodies, in accordance with their merits and previous deeds . . . ?" And in *De Principiis*, Origin seems to say that the soul has neither beginning nor end (III.iii.5). The soul passes through a succession of incarnations before eventually reaching God. This was based on the teachings of Plotinus, who maintained that even demons would eventually be reunited with God. Paul, writing to the Colossians, believed that all things would be reconciled with God (1:20). Augustine, in Book 1 of his Confessions, asked, "Did my infancy succeed another age of mine that dies before it? Was it that which I spent within my mother's womb? . . . And what before that life again, O God of my joy, was I anywhere or in any body?" Perhaps because of a belief in reincarnation, Augustine of Hippo (354–430 AD) could offer the prayer: "God grant me chastity and temperance, but not just yet." Augustine, incidentally, is the patron saint of brewers.

Synesius (370–480 AD), who was Bishop of Ptolemais, also offered a prayer: "Father, grant that my soul may merge into the light, and be no more thrust back into the illusion of earth."[2] The idea of life as illusion may seem as though it emanated from Eastern philosophy where the object of continuous incarnations was to end the cycle of rebirth.

There were, of course, other writers of this period, such as Tertullian who objected so vehemently against reincarnation that it may be indicative of how widespread the doctrine was. The primary reason why reincarnation became so prominent during this period was that belief in the imminent return of Christ had begun to wane and was replaced by increased Gnostic influence and Neo-Platonism with its body-soul dualism.

After Constantine made Christianity the official state religion, the church became enmeshed in the political arena and, because of a series of weak emperors, succeeded in influencing and controlling the operation of the empire. When Justinian put on the purple robe in 527, not only was the empire divided politically, but also religiously, as many minority expressions of the faith existed throughout the empire. Justinian was especially

2. Oderberg, "Reincarnation as Taught by Early Christians."

concerned about the Western church and the Bishop of Rome and convened the Council of Constantinople in 553 to suppress the influence of the Roman church. It was clear manipulation since the West was not represented. The Council approved (by a ratio of 3–2) fifteen anathemas directed against the Cathars, Albigensians, Waldensians who were influenced by Gnosticism and Origen. Origen was declared a heretic and Pope Virgilius, who was not present, was forced to accept the anathemas. In condemning these heretical groups and Origen, they were discarding the idea of the pre-existence of the soul and, therefore, of reincarnation.

Reincarnation was a threat to the authority of the church since it minimized the Christian doctrine of salvation by the grace of God. Salvation, in the theology of the church, was to attain entrance into heaven, or to be forever in the presence of God. This concept was one step removed from the Eastern thought of merging with the Godhead or being one with everything. The church renounced salvation by works and rejected the idea of a karmic return to try to get it right in succeeding lives.

Reincarnation was also in conflict with the resurrection of the body. Based on an interpretation of the Scriptures, the raising of Jesus was in bodily form. The church believed in "the resurrection of the dead," although Paul pointed out that the body which is raised may not be the body that had died. ("You do not sow the body that is to be, but a bare seed" [1 Cor 15:35–38]). Reincarnation also creates an unnatural separation of body and soul, which is more akin to Greek rather than Hebrew thought.

There was also the practical consideration that persons generally had no recollection of past lives. Except for poets and visionaries, reincarnation in western culture receded into the nether world of religious and philosophical thinking until relatively modern times. However, many famous individuals appear to have accepted reincarnation and/or recalled previous lives. The Renaissance philosopher, Giordano Bruno, was burned at the stake for his belief that souls pass from one body to another. Johann von Goethe said, "I am certain that I have been here as I am now a thousand times before, and I hope to return a thousand times." Henry David Thoreau wrote that he had lived in Judaea at the time of Christ, but never knew him. Mark Twain said in his autobiography, "I have been born more times than anybody except Krishna." Henry Ford adopted reincarnation at the age of twenty-six and said that work would be futile unless we can utilize it from one life to the next. Others who believed in reincarnation include

Born Again . . . and Again . . . and Again

Leo Tolstoy, Gustav Mahler, Ralph Waldo Emerson, Carl Jung, and General George S. Patton. There are many more.[3]

Children who had memories of a past life led Dr. Ian Stevenson to begin his study of cases suggestive of reincarnation. His first essay on past lives, "The Evidence for Survival from Claimed Memories of Former Incarnations," was published in 1960. What Stevenson looked for as he traveled an average of 55,000 miles a year between 1966 and 1971 was evidence of children's memories of persons or places not part of his life; specially formed birthmark corresponding to a scar which the former person received in connection with his death; similarity of personality characteristics. He also noted in these cases that there was an interval of less than ten years between death and rebirth, and that the death of the reincarnated person was generally intense or dramatic. The cases that Stevenson investigated did not involve famous persons. On the contrary, this made it more difficult because only a few friends or relatives knew the person.

Ian Stevenson's work was continued by Dr. Jim B. Tucker, a child psychologist who investigated accounts of children who remembered previous lives. Below is a list of frequent characteristics derived from these accounts:

1. Occurs most frequently in children 2–4 years of age.
2. Memories begin to fade at 5–8, as the child moves on to other interests.
3. Exhibits behavioral characteristics of the previous person or adult attitudes.
4. Describes the strangeness of a new body.
5. Past life memories are vivid, which also include historical events, e.g., James Leininger.
6. Violent death in previous life.
7. Phobias about cause of death (the only natural phobias are sudden sounds and falling); all others are learned. Other phobias and philias.
8. Observed changes in people and surroundings, e.g., "You lost your teeth!"
9. Announcing dreams predicting rebirth.
10. Abnormal appetites during pregnancy.

---

3. Cranston and Williams, *Reincarnation*, 62–68; Stevenson, *Twenty Cases*; Tucker, *Life Before Life*.

The Mysticism of Ordinary and Extraordinary Experience

11. Unusual and unlearned skills such as the ability to comprehend a foreign language.
12. Abnormalities of child-parent relationships; talk of an earlier mother.
13. Birthmarks often associated with the cause of the previous death; congenital deformities; birthmarks related to physical features of previous person.
14. Facial and other personal features related to previous person's identity.
15. Physical differences between monozygotic twins.
16. Addictions and unusual desires.
17. Apparent irrational aggression—national or racial vendettas.
18. Feeling of being the wrong sex.
19. Present behavior reflects past personality or idiosyncrasy.
20. Nostalgic longing for a previous family, e.g., Shanti Devi.
21. Recognition of persons from a previous life.
22. Games reflecting previous occupations, e.g., if your child plays at being an insurance actuary.
23. Sexual interest in a prior spouse. (Case of one person marrying his former spouse when he became adult.)

There are two modern cases that have been well-researched and reported and have aroused considerable interest in reincarnation. Sture Lonnerstrand, in his book, *I Have Lived Before: The True Story of the Reincarnation of Shanti Devi*, describes how a girl in the 1930s in India possessed such powerful memories of a former life that she was torn between her previous and present families.

One of the more recent cases of retrocognition that has achieved widespread attention is that of James Leininger, who remembers and resembles, James Huston, a World War II fighter pilot killed at Iwo Jima. This was detailed in the book, *Soul Survivor* by Bruce and Andrea Leininger.

Reincarnation as a system of belief appears in many of the world's religions and societies and the evidence for it seems to be overwhelming and persuasive. Nevertheless, other possible explanations have been offered, including made-up stories out of the fantasies of a child or information acquired through normal means which had been forgotten. There is also the possibility that those reporting the cases may have faulty recollections of the subjects' experiences and stories. Paranormal explanations, such as ESP and possession, have also been proposed.

One explanation is that of cellular memory, based on the hypothesis that the subject's cells hold the memories of past lives which can be activated by electrical impulses. The ancient Celts believed that the tribal memory of their ancestors could be retained not only within their bodies, but also within other living things, such as an oak tree. The Druids had the power to recall the memory of trees and were thus the repository of the tribal wisdom. Other stimuli could also trigger the release of stored memory.

Edmond W. Sinnott, in his 1955 study, *The Biology of the Spirit*, advanced the thesis that human aspirations are imbedded in the properties of protoplasm. In other words, the cells of the body have purpose and motive and possess a self-determination. The implication of this is that consciousness is not localized solely in the brain but pervades the entire living structure. One could advance to the next step and posit that memories from one life can be genetically transmitted. The problem is that many cases of recalled past lives were not related to the person whose life they had recalled. But if that theory were expanded to include the collective unconscious, then reincarnation may be a borrowing from the universal mind.

Death of a Young Girl in Springtime

MEDIA VITA IN MORTE *sumus*. "In the midst of life, we are in death." Thomas Cranmer translated this ancient antiphon and placed in the burial service in *The Book of Common Prayer*. Death often comes when we least expect it and shatters our hopes and dreams.

On a warm April morning, I sat in a small country church and listened to the quiet whispering of those who were gathering for the funeral service of a young girl who had just turned twenty-one the week before. She had died very suddenly of a brain hemorrhage while away at school. Colleen was the daughter of our Camp Manager of Properties. I knew her parents very well and have worked with them in the camping program of our church. I remember the year Colleen was born, just before the camping season began, and the joy that she brought to the lives of her parents.

And now just before another camping season was to begin, I was sitting in a church with more than 200 friends and relatives remembering her short life. Several thoughts came to me as I heard the words from the Revelation of John about the holy city, the new Jerusalem, coming down from heaven and the voice saying, "See, the home of God is among mortals" (Rev 21:3).

That little church was crowded—not with just relatives and members of the congregation—but friends from all over the Pennsylvania Southeast Conference—ministers, lay people, youth, conference staff—the whole church, all trying to share the burden of the hour with the family and in some way envelope them with the love of the Christian community. The "holy city" is the church, the community of the faithful, the company of believers, a family gathered to give witness that God was indeed present.

Too often we think of the church in terms of our own congregation gathered for worship, but here was a caring fellowship gathered to share pain and bring comfort. God dwelt in the midst of those people—for their presence, their prayers, their love, and their words of faith and assurance were testimony to the presence of the spirit of God.

As I listened to the sermon, other thoughts came as well. All lives are lived for a purpose. There is meaning to our being here. Sometimes that purpose is not for ourselves, but what we mean to others. Colleen's pastor raised the question of what her death meant in that her life was so short. It is not the brevity of life but the intensity of it—like a nova, a star that achieves its greatest magnitude, flooding the universe with light just before it changes its form. I thought of all the lives Colleen had touched and the meaning those lives will have because of her. We are all bound up together in this bundle of life and our lives do have meaning for one another. This is what John Donne meant when he said, "Everyman's death diminishes me, for I am involved in mankind" ("No Man is an Island"). We are all created of the same Spirit of God and it is intended that we should be involved with one another in a caring, loving way.

We came out of the church to a world that was alive with spring-time beauty. Green buds were bringing life back to a brown-gray forest. The earth was warm again and rich and ready for seed. It is winter that makes possible spring, the dark night followed by the light of day, the suffering which prepares the way for deepest insight and the greatest ecstasy—these are images of death and rebirth that are universal. Life is always being affirmed in the face of death. This is why the Prophet John could write a message of hope, of a new heaven and a new earth, all creation renewed, freed from imperfections, and transformed by the glory of God. This is why Paul could write: "I consider that the sufferings of this present time are not worth comparing with the glory that is to be revealed to us" (Rom 8:18).

We have gotten so used to looking at the negative side of life that we cannot see the potential for greatness. We have become so crisis-oriented that our sensitivity to the human condition is dulled. I get much of my news from broadcast media which has a habit of introducing important late-breaking stories with a kind of beeping noise that interrupts whatever happens to be going out on the air at the moment. Earlier that week I had been listening to the latest on the Iran situation when they interrupted the broadcast with a news bulletin. I was all set to expect another rescue attempt, or the release of the hostages, or a declaration of war. But no, it was none of that. They just wanted to tell me the earth-shaking news that a filly was going to be entered in the Kentucky Derby. We are being conditioned to expect the worst, and so we are unprepared when the news is not the worst.

The Mysticism of Ordinary and Extraordinary Experience

That is true of much of life. We will always find what we are looking for. If we expect life to be tragic, it will be. If we regard people as spiteful, greedy, and unloving, they will be. If we do not believe in God, God will not exist for us. How much do we shape our own realities and build the worlds we live in? If only we could see the world as God intends for it to be—to share in God's vision of the new heaven and the new earth.

As we left Colleen in that country graveyard, and to that realm of silence that separates our world from the next, I remembered the scene from Thornton Wilder's play, "Our Town," where Emily, who has died in childbirth, is given the opportunity to go back to a particular day in her past. She chooses her twelfth birthday. Thinking of the life she has lived and of her failure to appreciate its significance, she exclaims:

> It goes so fast. We don't have time to look at one another ... I didn't realize. So all that was going on and we never noticed ... One more look. Good-by. Good-by, world. Good-by, Grover's Corners ... Mama and Papa. Good-bye to clocks ticking ... and Mama's sunflowers. And food and coffee. And new ironed dresses and hot-baths ... and sleeping and waking up. Oh, earth, you're too wonderful for anybody to realize you.
>
> Do any human beings ever realize life while they live it—every, every minute? (3.3).

The answer is, "Of course not." So much of life is lost in the living of it. I wouldn't be surprised if the Last Judgment is the judgment we are forced to make on ourselves as we review our lives—the lost opportunities, the people we ignored, the causes we neglected to support, the words spoken in haste or in anger, the persons we failed to forgive or offended, the friend or relative with whom we remained unreconciled, the Christ whose presence we kept from our lives. Must we wait until we have passed into the next world to realize the opportunities we have in this one?

The Bible tries to teach us that heaven is a present reality as well as a future hope, but we seem too intent on preparing for the next life that we miss the meaning and purpose of this one—much like the American tourist in Paris who spends all his time reading the tour book and travel brochures about Rome, the next stop on the itinerary. Preparing for the future is important, but not when it prevents us from living in the present.

St. John promises a new heaven. Where is heaven? In his story, *The Fugitive*, the Indian writer, Tagore, tells of the father who returns home from the funeral of his wife.

Death of a Young Girl in Springtime

> His boy of seven stood at the window, his eyes wide open and a golden amulet hanging from his neck—a boy with thoughts too difficult for his age. His father took him in his arms and the boy asked, "Where is mother?" "In heaven," answered his father, pointing to the sky. The boy raised his eyes to the sky and long gazed in silence. His bewildered mind sent abroad into the night the question, "Where is heaven?" No answer came, and the stars seemed liked the burning tears of that ignorant darkness.

We live in a world of time and space, and therefore we tend to think of heaven in terms of location. In the realm of the spirit, there is no time, no space. The spiritual world exists in the midst of the physical world—it's a different kind of reality.

To the thief on the cross, Jesus promised, "Today you will be with me in Paradise" (Luke 23:43). But creatures who dwell in time do not know what "today" means to the dwellers of heaven. We can take comfort from the vision of John. But what does it mean to speak of streets that are paved with gold in a world in which things exist in a spiritual rather than a physical state? We cannot measure the New Jerusalem with an earthly yardstick. All we can do is trust in the God who offers us his presence in all possible worlds, Jesus speaks of heaven as a relationship with God. We experience heaven now when God's spirit is apparent to us. We experience hell when we deprive ourselves of God's presence.

The New Jerusalem is the church, and the message that the church bears to the world is that God is with us. The purpose of living is to enjoy the presence of God. We are not to seek the rewards of Paradise or avoid the torments of hell, but simply to know and love God.

This short prayer by the eighth century Sufi mystic, Rabia al-Adawiyah of Basra, summarized it well:

> O my Lord God, the stars are shining and the eyes of men are closed, and kings have shut their eyes, and every lover is alone with his beloved, and here I am alone with Thee. O my Lord God, if I worship Thee for fear of hell, burn me in hell. And if I worship Thee in hope of Paradise, exclude me from Paradise, but if I worship Thee for Thine own sake, then withhold not from me Thine eternal beauty.

Eternal life is to know God and when we know God, the former things are not so important after all.

Liminality at the Time of Death

Transitions of the Soul as a Rite of Passage

I HAVE ALWAYS HAD a fascination for doors. Doors marked transitional moments when you ceased being in one place and stepped into another, a clearly defined boundary between what was and what was to be. Doors not only marked spatial limitations, but also of time, and most especially, of the perception of reality.

Doors became a symbol of transition from this life to another long before. Moses ordered lamb's blood placed on the doorposts of Hebrew homes to spare them a visit from the angel of death. In Egypt it was common to place false doors, sometimes called the "Ka Door," in the tombs of the dead so that the *ka*, or spirit of the deceased, could return to have social interaction with the living and perhaps consume a glass of beer or wine.

The ancient Celts regarded doorways as a symbolic passage between the familiar and the unknown. The door was a protection of the social unit of the family or clan from the wider world with all its chaos and danger. The hanging of mistletoe over the threshold at the time of the winter solstice was intended to dissolve normal boundaries between two people, represented by the kiss, or between warring parties since mistletoe was a symbol of peace and the threshold was neutral ground where aggressive behavior and conflict were forbidden. There were also doors in the natural world, the so-called "thin places" of transparency, that enabled the "walkers between worlds" to experience another dimension of life and to seek answers to life's conflicts.

In the Gospel of John, Jesus refers to himself as the door, or the one who provides access to the spiritual realm, who reveals the nature of God. He is also the door of the sheepfold, and there are other folds, so that, according to some interpretations, the door provides interdimensional access

Liminality at the Time of Death

that unites all beings. And in Rome, the god Janus, the god of doors, is depicted with two faces, since every ending is also a new beginning. To embark on a new undertaking one must leave the past behind.

The critical part of the door is the threshold. The Latin word is *limen*. When you stand on the limen, you are between where you were and where you will be. You are neither here nor there. You are in a state of becoming. The University of Chicago anthropologist, Victor Turner, describes this marginality particularly with regard to rites of passage. Borrowing from the work of French anthropologist and ethnographer, Arnold van Gennep, Turner noted that all cultures celebrated transitions, whether seasonal or cycles of human development.

Van Gennep had described critical rites of passage in relation to the significant events of a person's life such as puberty, marriage, retirement, and death. Each event was characterized by three phases:

1. Separation, in which the person is set apart from his previous life and associations. In puberty rites, individuals can be covered in mud, a white robe, or some other form in which his previous station is obliterated, and he becomes an anonymous person, one of many undergoing the rite. Seasons were often marked by a procession indicating that one is moving from one point in the calendar to another, and that there was a clear demarcation in time.

2. Threshold or Liminal stage when one is neither what he was nor what he is yet to become. Turner felt that this was the most important phase. It was a time of upheaval and chaos where the rules of behavior of the previous life are suspended before a new contract with the social order is implemented. An example of this stage in the rite of passage would be that of the Amish custom of *rumspringa*, literally "running around." Amish teenagers are allowed to live outside the community and their faith to experiment with the world and all its decadence, including drugs, alcohol, sex, telephones, wild parties, and a college education. Once they have gone through this liminal period, they are now ready for the third stage.

3. Incorporation is the re-entry into a new world, a new social order, a new life. In marriage, the father and mother are left behind, and a new structure is begun. The Native American boy, in the liminal period, would spend nights in the sweat lodge to capture a vision of new life and discover his power animal, and then emerge to participate in the

hunt whereby he bonds with the men of his tribe. He is given a new name indicative of his new identity.[1]

The middle or liminal stage is probably the most important. This is Middle Earth, the "betwixt and between," the Twilight Zone, the shadow world between one form of existence and another. It is characterized by chaos and confusion, as well as revelation and insight. In the cycles of human civilization the fall of the Roman Empire, the Black Death, the Thirty Years War and its aftermath, and the Holocaust are just a few of these massive upheavals that plunged humanity into darkness before it was able to re-emerge into brighter days.

It was commonly believed that in liminal times the boundaries between worlds was so thin that sensitive persons such as mystics would more easily be able to interact with the spiritual world. In the same way, there were liminal times in the calendar, such as Walpurgisnacht, the eve before Beltane (May 1), when witches would gather for their rituals, and All Hallows' Eve (Halloween) the night before Samhain, when the spirits of the departed became more visible to dwellers of the physical world. Imbolc, celebrated in the New World as Groundhog Day, was the day when animals were consulted to determine if the natural world was ready to move on. Lughnasa, in midsummer, was a celebration of the beginning of the harvest season.

Liminality was not only a between-stage in time and space, it was also a period of transition and adjustment. When Elizabeth Kubler-Ross defined the five stages of dying, she was addressing the psychological process leading up to the moment of death. This would be analogous to Turner's and Van Gennep's initial stage of separation whereby the individual must sever his relationship with life as he had known it. As one moved from resistance to acceptance through the stages of denial and isolation, anger, bargaining, depression, it was a process of letting go of this life and looking forward to the life to come, or some cases nonexistence depending on one's religious perspective.

While Kubler-Ross described the process immediately preceding death, it was Raymond Moody, also a physician, who conducted studies of what persons encountered immediately following physical death. These studies, and those by Kenneth Ring and others, were based on anecdotal accounts of those who returned from the threshold of death, a retreat from the liminality of spirit. The criticism of these accounts of the so-called

---

1. Gennep, *The Rites of Passage*.

Liminality at the Time of Death

"near-death experiences" is that they are exactly that: "near-death," not death experiences. The medical definition of death is that you don't return from it. The brain ceases to function forever; the pulmonary process no longer works on its own; necrosis becomes universal and irreversible.

However, the preponderance of similarities in the anecdotal accounts of NDEs may give us insight into a greater dimension indicating the survival of consciousness into another existence. The belief in some form of postmortem existence is nearly universal, and in many cultures the mythology and religious beliefs and practices support a liminal period of transition from our current stage of existence to a life beyond the grave.

Forensic psychology cannot give us answers as to why Neanderthals covered their dead with red ochre, tied them into fetal positions, and placed them gently into pits facing the rising sun. One can only imagine that even at the dawn of civilization there might have been a respect for human life and the hope that there was something more beyond. Many ancient burials were provided with food for the journey to the afterlife, sometimes with weapons.

The Aboriginal peoples of Australia are among the most spiritually sensitive and have a long history of communication with their ancestors. They rely upon intuition and hunches and know intuitively when it is time to move the tribe from one place to another. "Dreamtime," where the time-space continuum is irrelevant, is the psychic or spiritual world. Here is where the records of all people are kept. This record, known as *Tjukurpa*, is also a form of energy that can be tapped into, usually at special places such as Uluru—or Ayers Rock as it has been called by the new people. The Aborigines believe that at death the person is transported to the sky and then returned to earth in a trance-like or dream state. Those who have a remembrance of this celestial excursion become shamans or spiritual guides for others in the tribe. There is a similarity to Native American groups and the Inuit people of Canada where the dead journey to the river of souls, the Milky Way, and then are reincarnated in another form. These journeys serve as transitional periods from one life to another where the former life is forgotten, and new knowledge is either gained or remembered and brought back for the benefit of others.

The Pyramid Texts, hieroglyphics found in the pyramid of Unas at Sakkara and dating around 2350 BCE, provide an understanding of the Egyptian view of the afterlife which was rooted in the cyclical nature of their physical world, the solar cycles, and the rising of the Nile. The

The Mysticism of Ordinary and Extraordinary Experience

Pyramid Texts are a collection of spells designed to ease the transition of the soul into the next life and give us our first glimpse into the Egyptian understanding of the afterlife. The texts were included in later tombs until they were supplanted by the Coffin Texts which became the basis for the Egyptian Book of the Dead.

Here also is a journey of the soul. When the ram-headed god, Khnum created the human fetus on a potter's wheel and then placed it within the mother's womb, he also created the *ka*, a spiritual shell which resembled the person and lived within the human heart. While the *ka* could separate from the body during times of deep sleep or coma in a form of astral projection (which occasionally could be seen by others), it was only at death that it became detached from the body. Because it was essential that the *ka* remain in close proximity to the body, the need for mummification became apparent. A *ka* statue was provided as a "spare body" in the event that the corpse was destroyed. Tombs became more elaborate with several rooms and even false doors to entice the *ka* to return following its nightly sojourn to be judged by Osiris. The Egyptian word for tomb was *het-ka*, or "house of the *ka*." Since the *ka* was a spiritual duplicate of the body, it was provided with food and water left at the false door. As long as the *ka* remained a viable entity sustained by the gifts of the living and the mercy of Osiris, the deceased held onto the possibility of eternal life.

There was also a nonphysical aspect of the person called the *ba* which contained the psychological essence of the individual, his personality and character, emotional disposition, and to some degree his intelligence. The *ba*, represented by a human-headed bird, also disconnected from the body at death and began its journey in search of the *ka*. The reunion of the *ka* and *ba* in the afterlife enabled the individual to become an *akh*, the spiritual body that continues to live through eternity. The survival of the *akh* is insured by the continued prayers of the priests and the descendants and in the existence of the name of the deceased. As long as the name existed in memory, prompted by the written cartouche in the tomb, survival in the afterlife was a certainty. The desecration of a tomb consigned its inhabitant to eternal death, thus the need for strict proscriptions in the form of strongly worded curses against potential grave robbers.

The ka was the essential container of the human identity, representing the soul of the person. The distinction between the *ka* and the *ba*, is akin to the difference between the *atman* and *prana* in Hinduism, and *ruach* and *neshama* or *nephesh* in Hebrew. Other terms from other cultures also refer to the life force of the individual such as the Hawaiian *mana*, Japanese *ki*, Chinese *chi*, or the Sanskrit *shakti*. Interestingly, several words referring to the life force derive from the same word meaning "breath" in their particular language.

There are several important themes that will surface in the Jewish and Christian concepts of creation and the afterlife: creation of body and *ka* by a potter-god, a spiritual journey or quest in the afterlife, the judgment of the human heart in the scales of justice, the dependence upon memory for survival and the power of the human name, and the creation of a spiritual body.

One other characteristic of Egyptian funeral customs was the incision into the nostrils that allowed the corpse to breathe. Breath contained the essence of life, and the dead were sometimes referred to as "those whose throats are closed." Without breath, there is no life. It was the god Re who held the *ankh* to the mouth of Pharaoh and gave him life. The combination of breath and name are a powerful expression of the life force, as evidenced in an inscription found in the tomb of Tutankhamun which reads: "To speak the name of the dead is to make them live again and restores the breath of life to him who has vanished."

The Egyptian influence on the religion of the Hebrews during their sojourn in the land of the pharaohs has been underestimated. Egyptian polytheism which embraced the deities of the Canaanite and surrounding cultures stood in marked contrast to Hebrew monotheism. However, one cannot help but speculate that, since the children of Abraham were living in Egypt during the Amarna period when Akhenaton was worshiping the Creator God, Aton, Yahweh's revelation to Moses on Horeb might be a natural progression. The similarities between Aton and Yahweh are extensive.

The Egyptian view of the afterlife was certainly much more complex and highly convoluted compared to that of the Hebrews. Unlike the Egyptians, the Hebrews in the pre-exilic period had little concept of the afterlife. Death was the final state of existence, and that was all that it was—simply being, with no sense of animation or purpose.

However, there is an image in the Apocalypse of John that appears in other cultures and traditions: a river or rivers seem to be boundaries that separate this life from the next.

In Revelation 22:1–2 John writes: "Then the angel showed me the river of the water of life, bright as crystal, flowing from the throne of God and of the Lamb through the middle of the street of the city. On either side of the river is the tree of life with its twelve kinds of fruit, producing its fruit each month; and the leaves of the tree are for the healing of the nations." The idea developed that the Christians, at the time of death, would gather at the river and cross over and there be met by the saints. Under the Dome of the Rock in Jerusalem, there is the so-called "Well of Souls," where some believe that the voices of the dead can be heard intermingled with the burbling sounds of the rivers of Paradise.

In the Celtic tradition of the Hebrides, death is the great unknown. According to the *Carmina Gedelica,* the archangel Michael accompanies us on our journey through life and the final passage of death known as the "river hard to see." Here also is a reference to being met by the sainted women in heaven, "stretching their arms for you, smoothing the way for you, when you go thither over the river hard to see." John Philip Newell, a leading authority on Celtic spirituality, compares these women to midwives who assist in the crossing of the river and those who bring forth new life from the waters of the womb. A Hasidic tradition says that in the waters of the womb we know from whence we came, but at birth we forget.

Stepping into the river is a forgetting of the previous existence, or as Turner would say, the first stage of separation. The river itself is the liminal stage, and the arrival on the other shore is the reintegration into a new life.

The prevailing myth of the Greeks said that the soul was liberated from the body at the time of death and then made its journey to the River Styx where the ferryman Charon would receive his obolus in payment for the transition to the next life in the realm of Hades. The living could not enter Hades without a passport, a golden bough, nor could those who were improperly buried, even if it were a handful of sand ceremonially placed over the corpse.

It was clear to the Greeks that you could not take the substance of this life with you. There were five rivers that separated the dead from the living, each river increasing the separation of the soul from the physical world. There was the Styx, whose name derived from the word for "hatred," where you abandoned any feelings of revenge, especially if you had died in battle or at the hands of an enemy. Acheron is the river or lake of woe, where all sorrows and regret are left behind. Cocytus is the river of wailing or mourning, where loved ones are left behind. Phlegethon is the river of fire that purged the soul of earthly things and the desire for material wealth. Finally, there is Lethe, the river of oblivion, from whose waters the dead drank to lose all memory of their former lives. One might be tempted to compare the Greek five degrees of separation to the five stages of dying outlined by Elizabeth Kubler-Ross as one prepares for the final transition of one's earthly life.

There are other images beside doors and rivers that serve as liminal points of transition. Jacob's dream at Bethel was that of a ladder connecting earth with heaven. He envisioned angels ascending and descending the ladder providing communication between the physical and the spiritual. Islam, which accepts the Old Testament as part of its heritage, recognizes the validity of Jacob's ladder. On Mount Moriah, it is claimed that the prophet Muhammad began his journey to heaven on a ladder of light or of gold, visiting each of seven levels of Paradise. Muhammad himself said that this ladder was "that to which the dying man looks when death approaches" (Quran 17).

Bridges and tunnels are also points of passage and represent transitional stages in the migration of souls. The Zoroastrian bridge, *Chinvat*, for example, was a hair's width, and those who were judged unworthy of Paradise plummeted into the fires of hell. In Islam, it is the *Sirat Bridge* over which the unrighteous must crawl, carrying the burdens of their sins, which becomes too much for them, and they, too, plunge into the eternal flames.

Christian views of the passage from this life to the next are diverse and sometimes complex. Based upon several interpretations of scripture, the dead are raised to new life and then judged on the basis of their actions, some to everlasting separation from God and some to the realm of heaven to dwell forever in the presence of God. The church added the concept of Purgatory as an intermediate step. Purgatory is where the not-so-good and the not-so-bad could be purged of their sins. Here again, this purgation was the process of separation from the past life and the removal of negative energies before the soul could enter Paradise.

Sukie Miller, founder and director of the Institute for the Study of the Afterdeath, in her book, *After Death*, describes four stages of the Afterdeath journey. Stage I is Waiting. Here is where the reality of death sinks in. It is the shadowland of earthbound spirits who do not know where they are, who roam the earth looking for guidance and direction, or who seek to complete unfinished business. Stage II is Judgment, where one's life is evaluated, either by the gods who impose an either-or sentence of heaven or hell, or the judgment one makes upon one's own life, usually with the assistance of a higher being. Stage III is what Miller calls Possibilities. It is the reward and opportunity segment where one goes on to the light, enters

The Mysticism of Ordinary and Extraordinary Experience

Paradise, enjoys the garden of joy and delight, partakes of all those forbidden pleasures denied on earth. It is the Elysian Fields, the Halls of Valhalla, and the fulfillment of dreams. It is whatever you want it to be. The Fourth Stage is that of Return, reintegration, reincarnation. One can tire of eternal pleasure, or seek to improve relationships, or return to guide others, or desire to achieve the ultimate goal of losing the self and becoming one with the universe.[2]

That which most exemplifies Turner's stages of separation, liminality, and return is *The Tibetan Book of the Dead* or the *Bardo Thodol*. The term "bardo" literally means a transitional or liminal state. The book is intended as a guide through the bardos, the forty-nine-day journey from death to rebirth. There are actually six bardo states, but because I would like to compare the bardos with Turner's stages, I will describe three of them.

The *Chikhai Bardo* occurs at the moment of death. Here the deceased person has a vision or insight of all-encompassing truth. The intention here is that when one realizes the greater existence, one forgets the life one has emerged from. However, only persons who have achieved the negation of the self can move on to Nirvana. Most remain in this bardo until they become aware that they have separated from their body. This may take a few days in which the person exists in a trance-like state without recognition of what has happened.

The *Chonyid Bardo* is the between state where judgment occurs. The person has a dreamlike vision where the person conjures mythical or semi-divine beings that force him to address the karmic residue of his previous life. All sorts of dream images will take place, such as the scales of justice in which black pebbles representing sins are weighed against white pebbles or good deeds. Here he may encounter Bodhisattvas or Buddhas who seek to help, or carnivorous demons and a jury of demigods ready to convict him for his evil ways. Of course, this is all illusion, the stuff of dreams, and if the person could realize and recognize it for what it is, then that person could move on to Nirvana.

The *Sidpa Bardo* occurs when the previous two bardos fail to accomplish the goal of achieving Nirvana. In this bardo, there is the return to physical life with all its degradation for the purpose of remediation. The process of rebirth continues until you get it right and break the cycle.

Dr. Raymond Moody, author of *Life After Life*, gathered an abundance of anecdotal material from persons who had a "near-death experience."

---

2. Miller, *After Death*, 61–161.

Liminality at the Time of Death

The points of commonality in these experiences are: hearing sounds such as buzzing; a feeling of peace and painlessness; having an out-of-body experience; a feeling of traveling through a tunnel; a feeling of rising into the heavens; seeing people, often dead relatives; meeting a spiritual being such as God; seeing a review of one's life; feeling a reluctance to return to life. You will notice several elements that are applicable to the stages of separation, liminality, and return, as well as historical and mythic accounts through the centuries.[3]

Moody's description of the tunnel of light is akin to that of Gustave Dore's illustration of "The Empyrean," from Dante's *Divine Comedy*, in which the tunnel actually consists of angels or beings of light diffusing into the greater light. One could also get the impression from this image of souls being drawn into the One, or that of mind becoming part of the Universal Mind.

In the analysis of the near-death experience, the person is confronted before moving on in the assimilation of souls, the point of no-return. The person is told by a familiar figure that it is not yet his or her time and then is told to return. One can only believe that if it were the person's time, the journey would continue through the tunnel until one loses one's identity in the heart of God.

In a cross-cultural study of over a thousand cases, Karlis Osis and Erlendur Haraldsson (*At the Hour of Death*) investigated what dying persons encountered at the portal of death. Most described the appearance of an apparition, sometimes of a living person, but mostly of someone who had previously crossed over. Often, it is a religious figure who is there to make the transition easier, or to accompany the person, or to relive one's memories. Sometimes, as in Moody's study, to send the person back.

I had the occasion to be present with several persons as they made their transition from this life to the next. Marvin's conversation with an empty chair in the oncological unit of the hospital and Katie's dream of her brother were both liminal moments when at the hour of death a person catches a brief glimpse of what is to come, or what one's beliefs have conditioned them to believe, will occur.

From what we know of persons when they die and from what we accept as evidence of postmortem survival, we can say that Victor Turner's three stage description of separation, liminality, and reintegration is appropriate. At the time of death, the person is prepared by psychological and

---

3. Moody, *Life After Life*, 29-31.

physiological changes that help him separate from the physical world. In the liminal stage he comes to the awareness that he is between worlds and must move in one direction or the other. In the third stage, he either returns to the physical or moves on to what his mind and belief-structure create for him. This can be an integration into a fellowship of souls or assimilation into God, the collective unconscious, Nirvana, Heaven, or whatever name he may use to describe it.

We have seen transitional stages many times in the natural world, for example, the larva, chrysalis, and imago stages of the butterfly. In the larger context, the cycles of birth, death, and rebirth are continually repeated. It will be the same in the greatest context of the expanding universe and the mind of God.

"I Told You So!"

In 1898, Morgan Robertson published his short novel, *Futility*, about an ocean liner named the *Titan* that crossed the Atlantic in April, collided with an iceberg and, because of the shortage of lifeboats, resulted in the deaths of many passengers. Fourteen years later, in April 1912, the *Titanic* sank under the same circumstances. There were so many other similarities between fiction and reality as to raise the question about the meaning of reality and the nature of premonitions. Indeed, Ian Stevenson recorded nineteen incidents of premonitions that had occurred to persons within two weeks before the Titanic disaster. (see also *Transcending the Titanic: Beyond Death's Door* by Michael Tymn.)

Whether it's Julius Caesar's wife or Abraham Lincoln or Adolph Hitler or Nostradamus, history is replete with accounts of advance warning of impending disaster. So widely accepted was the belief that persons can and do have foresight into events of a cataclysmic and traumatic nature that after the Aberfan Coal Disaster in Wales in 1966, the British Premonitions Bureau was formed. Correspondingly, a Central Premonitions Registry was created in New York. The purpose of both was to register the premonitions and precognitions of persons so as to discern a pattern and therefore create an advance warning network. It did not work as well as it was hoped since many people reported their dreams after the event, or because they were so personal and trivial as to be meaningless in a larger context.

While premonitions and precognitions are similar in that they give an indication of a future event, there are differences. Premonitions (Latin—*praemonēre* "to warn before") are more likely to be feelings, such as depression and uneasiness, about a future occurrence. Precognition is foreknowledge and is primarily a mental construct.

The Mysticism of Ordinary and Extraordinary Experience

Bonnie McEneaney, in her book *Messages: Signs, Visits and Premonitions from Loved Ones Lost on 9/11*, has collected sufficient anecdotal information from the survivors of those who perished in the World Trade Center disaster to validate the belief that there is a connection between persons that transcends this life. While McEneaney records observations of signs and portents that lead the survivors to believe that their loved ones still exist in some form, it is the detailing of the premonitions that is most interesting. In many cases it was not specific insight, but rather a sense of foreboding. In one case it was sufficient for one person, on his way to work, to turn around in Grand Central Station and arrive back home in time to see the collapse of the South Tower.

Several years ago, I visited the *aesclepeion* at Epidaurus where patients were placed in a drug-induced sleep known as *"enkoimesis,"* while snakes, sacred to the god Aesclepius, slithered around them. When they awoke, they told their dreams to the priest-physicians who then prescribed the remedy for their ailments. Occasionally, the dreams foretold other events in the lives of the percipients. Whether it was dream interpretation in ancient Egypt or Vision Quests in the sweat lodges of Native Americans, it is part of the human experience to seek and accept that which comes from beyond the dimension of sight and sound.

The nature of premonitions and precognition is under continuous scrutiny and I will leave it to scientists like Dale Graff to present a more detailed analysis of the phenomenon. Whether it is an aberration of the mind, or a warp in the space-time continuum, or a disturbance in the Force or Collective Unconscious remains to be seen. But it is not something to be ignored. When humans were more intuitive than empirical, our perspective on existence was not so limited. We will continue to be amazed at how humans process eternity.

The Future Is Not What It Used to Be

Arthur C. Clarke, the eminent inventor, futurist, and writer of science-fiction stories, including *2001—A Space Odyssey*, probably raised more questions than he intended in his 1953 short story, "The Nine Billion Names of God." In this story, the monks in a Tibetan lamasery believe that when all the possible names of God are written, the universe will end. The purpose of Creation would have been fulfilled. The monks hire computer technicians who develop a program for listing all possible names of God, and when the computer spits out the final name, "overhead, without any fuss, the stars were going out," confirming the observation that there is a last time for everything.

The purpose of existence, therefore, is to identify the nature of the Creator and the purpose for being. There is intentionality in the universe, a reason for our existence, and when the purpose of existence is accomplished, time will end. Of course, one of the problems with Clarke's story of the stars going out is that if it is God's intention, God must have planned it millions of years ago since it would take light years for earth to see the results.

Gene Roddenberry, the creator of the Star Trek universe, tackled the same issues of time and meaning. An avowed humanist, Roddenberry's concept of God was too great to be explained and appreciated by any one religion. In the film, *Star Trek: The Motion Picture*, the Enterprise crew encounters an alien space craft at the edge of the universe that is so vast that the earth starship can enter it and still navigate for days before reaching its center. This alien spacecraft has sent signals to earth looking for the Creator. Throughout the film we are led to believe that this is a religious search for the creator of the universe, but as Captain Kirk approaches the epicenter of the constantly expanding space craft named "V'ger," he realizes that he has come upon the twentieth century space probe "Voyager" that has, over the centuries, replicated itself and its intelligence and then sent out probes to find its creator. The Creator, as far as V'ger is concerned, is not a spiritual entity named God, but human beings. The arrival of the Enterprise crew satisfies V'ger's search for the Creator, since the Creator is incarnated in its creation.

Roddenberry's point is that which is created, if it is endowed with intelligence, artificial or otherwise, will seek out its creator. There is a desire or longing for living things to return to their source and to know the purpose of their being. The human question is, "Why do I exist, and am I fulfilling the purpose for which I am created?"

Inherent in both Clarke's and Roddenberry's stories, and that of so many other science-fiction writers, is the nature of time and its meaning for existence. Let us also explore some alternate concepts of time.

Linear time or existential time maintains that the present is the only reality. The past is memory, and the future hasn't happened yet. Some people like to live in the past because they know how it turned out. Modern quantum physics addresses the concept of retrocausality, of how the present can affect the past and thus revise the present.

The ancient Greeks had two words for time—*kronos* (passage of time, that which can be calibrated by chronometers), and *kairos* (time that is relevant, that has meaning). A biblical example might be from the book of Isaiah (6:1) when the prophet says, "In the year that King Uzziah died." This is *kairos* time. Modern scholars would speculate and use *chronos* time or 742 BCE.

While modern concepts of time usually involve cause and effect logic, the ancient Hebrews first perceived the effect and then determined the cause. The Biblical view of time is that events and actions were not confined to a moment and a location in the time-space continuum, but occurred for all time. For example, when the Old Testament prophets spoke on behalf of God, they were not merely addressing the issues of their day, but their words could be interpreted as applying to future events. Events happen and have meaning for all time.

There is also a holistic view—seeing time from a perspective outside of time—like flying in a plane and seeing where you were, where you are, and where you will be. If we are outside the dimension of time, we do not see it as individual points arranged in sequence, but as a gestalt, as a totality.

Many cultures such as the Egyptian, Babylonian, Mayan, and others saw a cyclical nature to time. Egyptians were aware of the continuity of time which was an endless repetition of the same thing. The Babylonians' sense of time was marked by constant rhythms or cycles of nature.

The Old Testament also recognized these cycles, or as Ecclesiastes 1:9 says: "What has been is what will be, and what has been done is what will be done; and there is nothing new under the sun."

Nevertheless, there was a teleology which recognized that these cycles were moving toward an end goal. The Apostle Paul in the New Testament said that all things in the end will be reconciled to God, will come back to its beginning, reminiscent of Isaiah 44:6—"I am the first and the last," and in the Apocalypse of John, "I am the Alpha and the Omega, the first and the last, the beginning and the end" (Rev 22:13).

We must be careful not to impose our worldview on the ancient world. While the ancients did not think in Einsteinian or quantum terms, there are indications that those terms may not have been that alien to them. While not thinking of time holistically, people over the centuries have attempted to predict the future. In the "Rubaiyat of Omar Khayyam," as translated by Edward Fitzgerald, is this verse:

> I sent my Soul through the Invisible,
> Some letter of that After-life to spell:
> And by and by my Soul return'd to me,
> And answer'd: 'I Myself am Heav'n and Hell

Heaven and Hell, past and future, the seen and the unseen, all lie within the mind or consciousness of the perceiver and using various devices one might be able to see or predict the future. These instruments of perception, such as staring into a pool of water, reading tea leaves, watching the flight of birds, crystal ball gazing, tarot cards, cleromancy, examining the entrails of animals, precognitive dreaming, and so on, were really efforts to suspend rational thinking and enter into another alternate state of consciousness. If one understands Carl Jung's "collective unconscious" whereby the totality of all consciousness, knowledge, awareness, etc., is in the mind of God, then it may be possible to access the mind of God. This would also be consistent with the theology of "panentheism," whereby the Spirit of God is in all things.

It is written in the Talmud that "A dream that is not interpreted is like a letter that is not read." In the Old Testament, God usually spoke to the prophets through dreams and visions that are referred to as the "dark speech" of God (Num 12:8), which is subject to interpretation. (God speaks directly with Moses so that the words are clear.)

The Mysticism of Ordinary and Extraordinary Experience

In modern times, going back to Sigmund Freud and Carl Jung, much has been written about dream interpretation. Montague Ullman and Stanley Krippner, working at the Dream Laboratory at Maimonides Medical Center in New York, did ground-breaking work in the area of telepathy and dreams. Dale E. Graff, former Director of Project Stargate, explored the nature of precognitive dreaming and other applications of parapsychological phenomena as part of a top-secret government program. I recommend his two books, *Tracks in the Psychic Wilderness* and *River Dreams*.

While divination occurs frequently in the Biblical texts, such as casting lots by means of the Urim and Thummim, the Deuteronomic code forbids its use outside the Hebrew faith. ("No one shall be found among you who makes a son or daughter pass through fire, or who practices divination, or is a soothsayer, or an augur, or a sorcerer, or one who casts spells, or who consults ghosts or spirits, or who seeks oracles from the dead. For whoever does these things is abhorrent to the LORD; it is because of such abhorrent practices that the LORD your God is driving them out before you." [Deut 18:10–12]). The reason for this warning is that one cannot be sure that the prediction is coming from the God who speaks to one's own consciousness, or if the divination is coming from an untested source. The question is whether one should act upon the prediction.

In the long history of the human habitation of this planet there have been hundreds, maybe thousands, of persons who have used the ability of precognition to see into the future and have proclaimed their insights. Seers such as Nostradamus, Edgar Cayce, Jeane Dixon, are among the most celebrated, but scientific experiments have shown that ordinary persons may possess the gift of precognition and clairvoyance. One wonders why statistically aircraft and trains destined for disaster had fewer people on board than others. In events such as 9/11, the Aberfan coal collapse, and the Titanic, there were many persons who had inexplicable premonitions and changed their plans at the last moment. J. P. Morgan was one who had such a premonition, but had an important meeting in the US. Fortunately, he received word that his meeting was canceled, so instead of boarding the Titanic he waited for a later voyage.

The West Side Baptist Church in Beatrice, Nebraska, exploded due to a natural gas leak five minutes after a scheduled choir rehearsal was to begin. However, no one was hurt because no one showed up for the event. Every one of the fifteen choir members had different explanations as to why they weren't there. They weren't necessarily premonitions, but ordinary reasons that delayed them. Is there a cosmic consciousness that gives meaning to all events and to all the destinies of all living persons?

When ancient peoples saw the repetition of events and recognized the cyclical nature of time, they may also have observed the nature of synchronicity or the coincidental occurrence of events. Two modern historical events are most prominent.

Abraham Lincoln and John F. Kennedy were both elected to congress and to the presidency exactly one hundred years apart (1846, 1860 and 1946 and 1960). Both were succeeded by a man named Johnson. Abraham Lincoln had a secretary named Kennedy and John Kennedy had a secretary named Lincoln.

And both presidents foresaw their own deaths. Lincoln told his bodyguard, Colonel William H. Crook, on the day he was assassinated that there were "men who want to take my life . . . And I have no doubt they will do it . . . If it is to be done, it is impossible to prevent."[1]

A few hours before he was shot, Kennedy allegedly said to his wife, Jacqueline, and Ken O'Donnell, his personal advisor: "If someone wants to shoot me from a window with a rifle, nobody can stop it, so why worry about it?"

There are so many other amazing similarities such as the sinking of the Titanic and Morgan Robertson's fictitious novel, *Futility, Or The Wreck of the Titan*, written fourteen years before the sinking of the Titanic and with an astonishing number of similarities.

The future is not what it used to be because it keeps on changing. It is not only affected by the events of the past and the present, but also by our evolving understanding of what the end result of space and time will be. The universe is alive and has many dimensions and states of being. The exploration will continue until we discover our unity in the Oneness of God.

1. Selzer, *Ghosts of Lincoln*, 162.

Time and Again

An English Heritage sign on a building in Kensington, London read: "Jacob von Hogflume, 1864–1909, Inventor of Time Travel, lived here in 2063."

I would like to have a conversation with him, but I'm afraid that the speed at which I am moving into the future will be inadequate to have a physical encounter in 2063. Of course, the sign is a joke perpetrated by Dave Askwith and Alex Normanton in their book, *Signs of Life*.

We are all time travelers moving toward the future, but the question is "can we go back to the past and return to the present day?" Following the publication of Albert Einstein's "General Theory of Relativity" in 1916, *Punch* magazine in 1923 included this limerick:

> There was a young lady named Bright
> Whose speed was far faster than light;
> She set out one day
> In a relative way
> And returned on the previous night.

Einstein speculated that space-time is curved due to the effects of gravity of large celestial objects. If time is affected by gravity and is warped, then there exists the possibility that it could have an effect on a person or the consciousness of a person.

Time travel to the past might be theoretically possible in certain general relativity space-time geometries if one could move faster than the speed of light. Scientists talk about cosmic strings, transversable wormholes, Alcubierre drive, and other speculative theories emanating from quantum physics.

This opens up a worm hole into the concept of parallel universes or alternate realities that co-exist with our own where paradoxes can be explained, and the appearances of ghosts and other non-physical manifestations can become plausible. History, as well as the sacred writings of many cultures, is replete with accounts of seers and visionaries who see the future with remarkable clarity. We also have an abundance of accounts of persons who say that they have experienced encounters with persons known to have existed in another time.

In his autobiography, *Dichtung und Wahrheit*, the great German author, Johann Wolfgang von Goethe describes riding on horseback to the village of Drusenheim and encountering himself riding toward him. The *doppelganger* was wearing different clothes, but it was clearly Goethe. Eight years later, Goethe found himself returning from Drusenheim attired, quite by accident, in the same garb he had seen earlier. He does not say whether he encountered the Goethe that had perceived him eight years earlier.

These juxtapositions of time are not only fascinating but push the frontiers of rational thought and compel theories that are on the edge of scientific investigation. Yesterday's fiction becomes today's theory and tomorrow's truth. However, when we get right down to it, we are still using the mind as perceiver and knower.

Years ago, I learned the principle of "what you perceive is what you conceive, and what you conceive is what you create." The universe is created out of the mind of God but is apprehended by the human mind. The science-fiction writer Robert Heinlein used the term "pantheistic solipsism"—we create parallel universes by imagining them. Thus, Oz or Narnia or Mordor are real.

It is easy to dismiss paranormal studies as fantasy, time displacement as paradoxical, or the appearances of spiritual entities as psychosis, but if Heisenberg's Uncertainty Principle is correct, the universe, or multiverse, changes just by observing it.

Sacred Places

During the time of early adolescence, a Native American boy would make a journey into the wilderness. He would begin his vision quest with a ritual of purification in the sweat lodge and then continue to seek self-knowledge and insight through communion with the natural world. He might watch a flower unfold in the morning mist or listen to the language of frogs around a pond at dusk. The stars would stoop low to whisper the secrets of the heavens, and the power of the earth would rise up through the soles of his moccasins. The Great Spirit would tell him his name, and he would know who he was. It was a time of knowing and a time of becoming.

The call to my vision quest did not begin in a sweat lodge, but on a hot and steamy Sunday afternoon in August. Pastor Matt Theis appeared at my apartment at 1:00 and said, "You're going to church camp. I'll be back for you in an hour. Get your things together."

Earlier that year, I had won first place in my church's "stewardship" contest by writing an essay on how church contributions are used to send needy kids to summer camp. My prize was an eight-dollar subsidy toward the cost of going to camp. I had forgotten about it until Pastor Theis called.

The automobile drive was an odyssey in itself—from my urban civilization of paved streets to Pennsylvania, land of cows and bears. Two older girls, Gail Schnegelberger and Lillian Litwitz, rode in the back, speaking their girl-talk to each other. I sat up front with the pastor. I had packed a few comic books to relieve the anticipated boredom of church camp, but they were in the trunk. There was nothing up front to pass the time except to talk with the pastor or to read his Bible. I had nothing to say so I opened the book. It was enough to earn a pat on the back from the minister.

We stopped at the Lambertville Hotel for dinner. By now it was dark, and one could barely see the bridge that would take us across the storied

Sacred Places

Delaware River into the state my relatives always referred to as "the sticks." I had a feeling this was to be my last good meal for a week.

Matt Theis stopped off somewhere near Doylestown to visit a seminary classmate and get directions to the camp. They chatted while we waited. It was already after eight. It would be another two hours before we finally found our way to Camp Fernbrook, just outside of Pottstown. We pulled up to the darkened Lodge. The pastor turned off the engine, and we got out. And then it hit me.

Total terror. This was primal fear. Here I was in the middle of a dense forest. Not one glimmer of light and absolute quiet except for this strange chirping sound that seemed to come from everywhere. The city at least had streetlights and the comforting sound of traffic and police sirens, and the occasional roar of an airliner landing at Newark Airport. I never expected anything like this. I got back in the car and waited.

A light soon appeared in the distance and moved toward us. It was the camp director's flashlight as she made her way back from checking the cabins. "We've been expecting you," she said, "Did you get lost?"

That was an understatement. Pastor Theis abandoned me to my counselor who welcomed me to the Oaks, a large cabin divided into three sections. I was assigned to Pin Oak on the upper level. I was later to learn that the girls were scattered in smaller, individual cabins because there were more of them. But I overheard one of the counselors say that the boys were confined to Oaks because they could control them better.

Camp was not as bad as it seemed. My counselor was a seminarian named Bruce Hatt who seemed to spend more time with a kitchen girl named Millie than with his campers. Bruce and Millie eventually got married, and Bruce became the head of East Penn Camps. He was my predecessor at St. John's Church before moving on to a pastorate in Las Vegas. He was a gutsy kind of guy who wouldn't hesitate at breaking the mold of the pastoral image. I liked him, and I still have on the shelf of my study his treasured instrument for making important decisions—a pair of dice from the Flamingo Casino.

The fear of the first night soon passed, and I began to recognize the special beauty of the camp and the accepting and encouraging nature of the staff. We were taught that each day must begin and end with an encounter with the divine. One begins the day in the solitude of the "Morning Watch" and ends in the community gathering on Vesper Hill and final prayers at "Lights Out."

The Mysticism of Ordinary and Extraordinary Experience

For a boy who was raised in the city there are sights and sounds in the woods that are awesome—that fill you with awe and wonder. You are amazed at the simplicity of it all, and then at closer view, the complexity of the natural world. A morning mist hovering over a pond; the flight of birds in the setting sun; a camp fire circle opening to the heavens in which the ascending sparks merge with so many stars that one could scarcely look at them without tears of utter awe streaming down your face. There is a sense of the Holy, of God infused in every rock and tree and blade of grass, speaking in every waterfall, bird call, and breeze through the leafy trees. It was my vision quest, for now I knew who God was, who I was, and what I wanted to become.

Or so I thought. The vision quest is a journey, but the road always loops back to where one lives. There is nothing but the memory, but that is enough to change you for a lifetime. When Peter, James, and John went on a vision quest to the Mount of Transfiguration, they wanted to remain there, savoring the exalted moment of transcendence in the presence of God. But Jesus said that the journey to the mount of mystical encounter is not complete until one returns to where one lives.

I returned to Newark and tried to find my holy places in the city. The river was a powerful image from the Bible. We sang "Shall We Gather at the River" and "Deep River." Though I had not yet read the book, Thomas Wolfe's *Of Time and the River* sat on the family bookshelf, and I thought of that "ever-rolling stream that bears all its sons away" into some vast ocean. A pristine river of crystal-clear water flowing from a virgin mountain spring to nourish and sustain the children of God as they cavorted in a golden meadow with azure skies above—what a beautiful image.

All I had was the Passaic River. I sat along its shore and watched its murky black and brown water flow by into eternity as its gentle ripples deposited congealed petrol, dead fish, broken bottles, and the detritus of sex at my feet. Where were the virgin waters?

I sought the wilderness experience, a place of solitude apart from other humans where I might commune with nature and with God. All I could find was an oak tree in Independence Park. But it was the largest tree in the park and surrounded by heavy shrubbery. I often went there and stood with my back to the tree, feeling its energy, strength, age, and wisdom. I whispered my prayers to God for those I loved, thinking, and perhaps hoping, that somehow the tree would be my witness. I am sure that had anyone followed me, they would have thought that my rendezvous

Sacred Places

with the oak and the whispered conversations would make me a Druid of the first order. It wasn't quite Morning Watch or Vespers, but it was enough. I felt in touch with God.

Rudolph Otto, in his book *The Idea of the Holy*, talks about the *mysterium tremendum*, "that which is quite beyond the sphere of the usual, the intelligible, and the familiar . . . filling the mind with blank wonder and astonishment."[1] It inspires a holy awe or wonder.

The closest I ever came to this as a child was in the planetarium of the Newark Museum. It was a special place, more sacrosanct than any church. One entered in a semi-darkness that compelled one to speak in hushed tones as though something marvelous was going to happen. The anticipation was heightened as the rosy hue of dusk gradually faded to black, and the "oohs" and "aahs" of the audience betrayed the wonder and majesty of a night sky unseen in the smog and pollution of the Newark heaven.

And then the narrator spoke, and it was like the voice of God: "This is the universe. And we are a minuscule part of it." Virgil was about to take me on a tour of Paradise and for forty-five minutes, I was no longer an earthbound spirit. The vastness of space was described in numbers so large that only God could imagine them. But when the narrator spoke of our sun as a star that would burn itself out in so many billions of years, I became afraid—as though I might actually be a witness to that cosmic event, or even care.

The Newark Museum was my place of refuge, one of the holy places in the city along with the Van Buren Branch Library, St. Stephan's Church, and the sacred oak in Independence Park. Later, when I ascended to a higher level of consciousness and could afford the bus fare, the Metropolitan Museum of Art and the American Museum of Natural History in New York City became the goals of my weekly vision quests.

The Newark Museum was a good place for kids. On the first floor, they had some nice pictures on the walls that you had to walk past to get to the good stuff. The Children's Museum was in the back with the planetarium. No one ever visited the second floor, and yet it was here that some of the holiest artifacts were located. I did not learn until much later that the Newark Museum houses one of the finest collections of Tibetan art in the country.

The third floor contains the most interesting items. Here were the dinosaur fossils and stuffed animals, and one of the best mineralogical exhibits anywhere. Later, when I was in my teens, I worked in the mineralogy

---

1. Otto, *Idea of the Holy*, 26.

The Mysticism of Ordinary and Extraordinary Experience

lab running tests to identify specimens that were brought in from various field trips.

I worshiped the gods of science and knowledge and made my sacrifices at the altar of learning. One memorable sacrifice occurred in early December. It was near closing time and a light rain had started to fall. I wanted to get to the bus stop and get home before the rain increased. As I walked past the gift shop, my eye caught a little book on astronomy. I stopped to leaf through it. I had to have it. "A Field Guide to the Stars" it said, and it had pictures of all the planets and constellations and comets and meteorites. It was wonderful, and it only cost a dollar.

One dollar was all I had, and it meant that I would have to walk home. I gave it a moment's thought, but there was no real choice. I bought the book with my bus fare and began the four-mile walk in the rain.

Unfortunately, the rain started to freeze and turned to sleet. When I got home, there was a thin coating of ice on my wool coat, but the rain had soaked through. I was thankful that there was a plastic coating on my star book.

Mom got out the Vick's and camphor, boiled some water, and mixed it in a bowl. I sat at the kitchen table with a towel over my head and my face in the steaming bowl, the white man's version of the sweat lodge.

I hated it, that is until I thought of the Delphic sibyl whose visions guided the ancient Greeks. She would sit on a tripod breathing in the noxious vapors to see the will of the gods. Could I receive such visions from breathing Vick's? All I got was pneumonia. A little learning can be a dangerous thing.

What I have learned, though, is that life is the accumulation of the insignificant, that when taken in its entirety affects one's direction and one's life. A pat on the back for opening a Bible; the kindness of an understanding mentor; all the sacred places and wise sages met along the way—they are all the fulfillment of one's destiny. Moses should never have put his sandals back on, for holy ground would be forever under his feet. Sacred places are wherever a person encounters God and confronts the reality of who he is.

From Deep to Deep

It was early evening when our ship left port at Southampton. I was looking forward to the voyage to St. Petersburg in Russia, the country that my grandparents had left before the revolution to begin a new life in America. In a way, this was to be a voyage of discovery, not only of visiting new ports, but of rediscovering meaning in old memories. The only reason for revisiting the past is to see what it can tell you about who you are and what your future might be.

The light was beginning to fade by the time we entered the English Channel and the North Sea beyond. I stood alone on the deck and watched the lights along the shore. Channel traffic was quiet that night as we sailed past Dover Beach. I could not help but think of Matthew Arnold's poem, "Dover Beach":

> The sea is calm to-night.
> The tide is full, the moon lies fair
> Upon the straits;—on the French coast the light
> Gleams and is gone; the cliffs of England stand,
> Glimmering and vast, out in the tranquil bay.

Whether it was the rhythmic sound of the ship's turbines or some other cadence, I felt the "eternal note of sadness" that Sophocles long ago heard on the Aegean. I did not want to think of human misery, but this was not the first time the ocean spoke in a language only the soul could hear.

I had sailed on the Aegean several times, crossing the paths once plied by Odysseus and Jason and Themistocles. It was on the Saronic Gulf, en route to the isle of Aegina, that I also heard the voice of the deep. In another life I might have said that it was the whispering of Poseidon, but now I understood it to be the voice of my God calling me to new experiences and new memories that would shape my being. Odysseus heard it too so long ago. He knew to stop the ears of his crew with wax so that he alone could hear the sirens' alluring call that summoned him to ecstasy—and to danger.

The Psalmist, who often voiced his laments from the pit of despair, would say, "Deep calls to deep at the thunder of your cataracts; all your waves and your billows have gone over me" (Ps 42:7). Only that which is deep within you can speak with meaning to your life. The Psalmist knew that God was deep within him, and that he had to seek that still, small voice of calm in order to hear God's voice of presence and solace.

Dietrich Bonhoeffer, who died on the gallows in the Flossenburg concentration camp, heard the sirens' voice of God and said in *The Cost of Discipleship*, "When Christ calls a man, he bids him come and die." When you hear that voice from the depths, you find within you a peace that will enable you to face even death with calm and the assurance that you are safe in the sea of God's love.

I have often looked for places near the ocean for those brief sabbatical times to rest, reflect, re-energize, and re-cast the direction of my life. Mostly it would be some quiet beach, some isolated section in Wrightsville Beach, North Carolina. We had vacationed there most summers for some thirty years, thanks to Mary Ann's brother, Bill, an engineer who retired from General Electric in Wilmington where he had last worked. He had a house on the Intracoastal Waterway where he could moor his boat. It was a short drive down South Lumina Avenue where the ocean enters Greenville Sound. Years ago, it was a desolate section with very few beachgoers. A place to be alone. A place to which I always long to return.

Having grown up in Newark, New Jersey, we looked forward to summers "down the shore," anywhere from Asbury Park to Wildwood. We could always find someone who had a bungalow where we could crash. But the Jersey shore was noisy. So noisy that you couldn't hear the ocean in a conch shell, let alone the sound of waves pounding surf. The natural sounds of the sea were overwhelmed by the human cacophony of children, transistor radios, yelling lifeguards, and Frisbee players. I was only exchanging the noise of the city for the noise of resorts and boardwalks.

The Passaic River did not feed my soul. It was more of an open sewer with its wretched refuse teeming on its shore: beer cans—cheap Thunderbird and other rotgut whiskey bottles, condoms, and various other remnants of sordid pleasures. The life in its waters was limited by its toxicity, but it would eventually merge with a vast ocean and become alive again.

From Deep to Deep

Earlier in my life when I was small, my concept of God was also small and somewhat limited. I have come to believe that consciousness, my awareness of the universe, is not simply the product of my physiology, but transcends my body and is only facilitated by the parts of my brain. My consciousness is only a part of an infinite sea to which it will return.

I guess I was becoming a Gnostic even before I knew what a Gnostic was. Plotinus, Origen, and Pseudo Dionysus the Areopagite all said some things that started to make sense to me. I wondered about *apocatastasis*, and whether the Apostle Paul in his letter to Colossians (1:20) really meant that all things would be reconciled to Christ through the blood of the cross. But was there a limit to God's grace? Martin Luther thought so. He couldn't believe that the devil and his angels could ever come back to God. That bothered me because it brought into question the sovereignty of God. After all, how could an omnipotent deity possessing absolute love not overcome evil by grace alone? Were there limits to *sola fide* and *sola gratia*, faith and grace alone, that would exclude the forces of evil? The river gave me too much to think about.

But it was a place to be alone and yearn for other places to contemplate the lives I wished I could live and the person I was hoping to become. I knew that somewhere up north in Morris County the Passaic had its origins in a relatively unpolluted pond, but after crashing over the Great Falls in Paterson it picked up more of the industrial and human waste before making its way into Newark Bay and New York Harbor. But unlike the ever-flowing stream that bears it all away, the dream was not forgotten upon the dawning of a new day. New dreams would flow and hopefully they would be unpolluted by time. It was, however, a necessary river in my life, for one must be aware of all that flows through it as it courses to its destination.

The ocean at Wrightsville Beach had its own pulse and rhythm. There were moments when I would be transfixed by the monotony of waves ebbing and flowing, creating their own patterns in the world of my awareness. The sea not only contains an amazing abundance of living things, but is indeed life itself. With apologies to the biblical myth of the Garden of Eden, most scientists believe that life on this planet emanated from the ocean. Nevertheless, I give the writers of Genesis some credit for recognizing the importance of water in the creation of life. The wind, breath, creative force of God moved over the abysmal waters and separated them from the dry land. And the word "Eden" may have derived from an Aramaic word meaning "well-watered." The pre-scientific mind of the writer no doubt

The Mysticism of Ordinary and Extraordinary Experience

recognized water as the source and sustainer of life, for indeed Eden was watered by four rivers, the Pishon, Gihon, Tigris, and Euphrates.

Some paleo-biologists believe that human life evolved from primitive forms that began as cells in a vast primeval ocean some four billion years ago, speculating that surface conditions then were not conducive to sustaining life on dry land. More recent studies by some scientists may indicate that life began in primal mud in ponds enriched by the right kind of chemicals. That certainly would be consistent with the Genesis account of God scooping mud from the earth and breathing in the divine *ruach* or breath to create humans.

Nevertheless, regardless of whether life emanated from the deep sea or from pond scum on dry land, water was definitely a key ingredient.

President John F. Kennedy, who so much enjoyed sailing in Nantucket Sound, once said at an America's Cup Dinner, "I really don't know why it is that all of us are so committed to the sea, except I think it is because in addition to the fact that the sea changes and the light changes, and ships change, it is because we all came from the sea. And it is an interesting biological fact that all of us have, in our veins the exact same percentage of salt in our blood that exists in the ocean, and, therefore, we have salt in our blood, in our sweat, in our tears. We are tied to the ocean. And when we go back to the sea, whether it is to sail or to watch it we are going back from whence we came."

Human life begins in water, in the amniotic fluid of the womb, and our bodies consist of up to sixty-five percent water. (No wonder I sometimes feel like I am drowning.) And of course, in the amniotic universe of the womb it is much higher. Here is where we are secure, nurtured, protected from the outside world, and closer to God.

One of my favorite poems is William Wordsworth's "Intimations of Immortality." He speaks of the emergence from the darkness of the womb into the light of a new existence.

> Our birth is but a sleep and a forgetting:
> The Soul that rises with us, our life's Star,
>   Hath had elsewhere its setting,
>   And cometh from afar:
>   Not in entire forgetfulness,
>   And not in utter nakedness,
> But trailing clouds of glory do we come
>   From God, who is our home:
> Heaven lies about us in our infancy!

From Deep to Deep

> Shades of the prison-house begin to close
>   Upon the growing Boy,
> But he beholds the light, and whence it flows,
>   He sees it in his joy;
> The Youth, who daily farther from the east
>   Must travel, still is Nature's priest,
>   And by the vision splendid
>   Is on his way attended;
> At length the Man perceives it die away,
> And fade into the light of common day.

In many ways, water is the source of life. It is also the sustainer of life. For a desert people the withholding of water could be a criminal offence; it would certainly be a violation of the laws of hospitality. In many gospel stories, the enmity between Jews and Samaritans was very great. Samaritans were not permitted to offer hospitality to Jews, so it seemed strange to the woman at Jacob's well at Sychar for Jesus to ask for a drink of water. This biblical account presents water as an archetype for that which sustains life.

It was interesting that whenever I visited with a Muslim family in Jerusalem, after the usual expression of *"As-salamu alaykum"* ("peace be upon you"), I was offered a glass of water. (Although in Turkey, my secular Muslim friends would offer me a glass of *raki*.)

Water also came to symbolize renewal and cleanliness. At various archaeological sites in Israel, *mikva'ot* were common. The *mikveh* was used not only for ritual cleaning, but also for converts to Judaism to represent a new spiritual life. It was a restoration to wholeness, one meaning of the commonly used word *shalom*. At the Pools of Siloam and Bethesda and even on Mount Masada are evidence of the importance of the *mikveh* in Judaism. This ritual was transformed into Christianity by Jesus who was baptized by his cousin John in the Jordan River.

There was a River Brethren preacher who would baptize his born-again believers by holding them under the water for a longer time than seemed necessary. As the repentant sinners would emerge gasping for air, he would remind them to desire God as much as they desired air to breathe. There is something about being immersed in a river and then coming up to breathe again. One appreciates the renewal of life. It is no wonder that the old gospel song, "Down to the River to Pray," made famous by Alison Krauss' version in the movie, "O Brother, Where Art Thou?" may have derived from an old slave song that promised freedom. Like so many of the spirituals, such as "Steal Way," "Follow the Drinking Gourd," "Wade in the

The Mysticism of Ordinary and Extraordinary Experience

Water," the songs contained coded information to help slaves on the Underground Railroad to find freedom. Going down to the river to pray also helped the slaves by covering their scent so as to elude the bloodhounds of the bounty-hunters. "Good Lord, show me the way," was not just a plea to gain the robe and starry crown, but a heartfelt longing to go north to a new life. The drinking gourd was the Big Dipper, and the starry crown was the constellation *Corona Borealis*, both in the northern sky.

I savored those times at the beach watching the rhythmic and gentle waves touching the shoreline. It had a way of restoring my soul. But the sea was not always calm. There were times when Poseidon would raise his trident in anger, and the ocean would rise up in a raging force to bring death and destruction.

As I am writing this, Hurricanes Harvey, Irma, and Marie have already visited Texas, the Caribbean, and Florida with lethal force. Water that brings life and healing can also come with pain and suffering. I am reminded of the Deuteronomic words of God, spoken in a different context, "See, I am setting before you this day a blessing and a curse, life and death. Therefore, choose"

Sometimes we don't have choices. We call it the vicissitudes of life, accidents, pure chance. But it may not be so. Whether we label it karma, destiny, fate, or the hand of God, there is intentionality in the universe, all things may occur for a purpose. The tide that comes in will eventually go out. The sea is always in motion.

The sea has taught me to be patient with life. That which destroys can also create. That which sets us apart from another can also generate waves of human compassion as neighbors nearby and around the world make sacrifices to help one another.

From the waters of creation to the waters of re-creation (and recreation), water is life. The ocean helps me to recognize that we all come from the same source and will return to that common consciousness. We are all part of the oneness of God.

American Poustinia

IN THE FOURTEENTH CENTURY, the Bubonic Plague annihilated more than one-third of the population of Europe. The Black Death, as it was also called, introduced by flea-bearing rodents, created such a massive social, religious, and economic catastrophe that it took almost two centuries for Europe to recover.

This late Medieval period was also known as the age of the mystics, especially women who were sensitive to and often overwhelmed by feeling the love of God. Some withdrew from society and took refuge within the cloistered walls of the church. Others sought to be the presence of God among the poor, suffering, and downtrodden of society. The plague years had a profound influence on two women in particular.

Julian of Norwich (1343–c.1422) adopted the practice of social distancing and "sheltering-in-place" when she became an anchoress, or hermit, who lived in a small cell attached to the church in Norwich. Here she spent her life in solitude, silence, and contemplation where, devoid of distractions, she could be aware of the presence of God.

Her often quoted phrase, "All shall be well, and all shall be well, and all manner of thing shall be well," is often assumed to be an optimistic self-delusion to cope with the calamities of her day—war, plague, immorality, sin in all its forms, both within the church and in society in general. But Julian took the longer view and believed that the goodness of God will eventually prevail and that God's amazing grace will lead us through all the perils of life. She referred to God as clothing that protects us, embraces us, and surrounds us with love. Julian wrote about sixteen of her visions, or "shewings," in one of the first books written by a woman, *Revelations of Divine Love*, which is a classic of Medieval church literature.

No doubt, Julian was familiar with Psalm 91, sometimes referred to as the Psalm of Plagues, which is used as a prayer of deliverance, particularly

The Mysticism of Ordinary and Extraordinary Experience

in times of plague such as the twenty-first century outbreak of coronavirus. The psalmist says that you will find refuge under God's wings so "you will not fear the terror of the night, or the arrow that flies by day, or the pestilence that stalks in darkness, or the destruction that wastes at noonday" (Psalm 91:5-6). Julian believed that rather than delivering us from the times of peril by avoiding them, God's love would carry us through the storms of life. As God had said through the prophet Isaiah, "When you pass through the waters, I will be with you; and through the rivers, they shall not overwhelm you" (Isa 43:2). Winston Churchill said during the Second World War, "When you are going through hell, keep going." Julian's faith in the abiding presence and love of God convinced her that all shall be well. One must trust God, be patient, and endure.

While Julian retreated from the world to become an anchoress confined to a small cell where she could contemplate the presence of God, others like Catherine of Siena (1347-1380) sought God in service to those affected by the Black Death. Mysticism is not complete separation from the world. The mystical life calls one to see God involved in humanity. It recognizes the Divine in humanity and in all creation. The true mystic pursued direct communion with God and experienced that communion in service to others in whom they saw the presence God. Mother Theresa of Calcutta is an example of a modern mystic. She saw the face of God in the poor, the sick, the dying, regardless of their religion.

Catherine of Siena was a prolific letter writer. Like Hildegard of Bingen, she communicated with bishops, cardinals, the pope. But her communication with Jesus framed her entire life. She recorded these conversations in a book which she titled *The Dialogue*. She would ask Jesus questions, and he would answer her. One of the questions, for example, was why Jesus' heart was pierced on the cross when he was already dead. Jesus replied that while suffering is finite, he wanted to show by means of the opened heart that his love for humanity was infinite (*The Dialogue*, chapter 6). Jesus further told her that she must love others with the same love that he had for her and all persons.

That love would also cause her to experience rejection and abuse from those to whom she tried to demonstrate of love of Christ—plague victims, lepers, prisoners, the poor and oppressed. We see examples of this in our time in the many doctors, nurses, caregivers, and others who tirelessly work to bring aid and comfort to modern victims of pandemic. God's love is continually made real in our lives.

American Poustinia

Catherine tried to mitigate the controversy in the church by writing to Pope Gregory XI and urging him to return to Rome. It was the beginning of the Great Schism, and when Gregory died, Catherine went to Rome to help the new pope, Urban VI. Worn out from all the trials and tribulations of the times, Catherine died at the age of thirty-three.

Like Dietrich Bonhoeffer who died on the concentration camp gallows, Catherine of Siena and many others who responded to the call of Christ were prepared for suffering and even death; for indeed, as Bonhoeffer wrote, "When Christ calls a man, he bids him come and die."

However, throughout the course of Christian history there were many religious who desired to escape from the sins of the world, the trials and travails of human interaction, and the distractions of involvement in political and social discourse. They were called by many names—hermits, eremites, anchorites, cenobites, monastics, ascetics, hesychasts, poustiniks—which indicated various degrees of withdrawal, practice, and purpose. Many of these terms derive from the early days of Christianity when persons would retreat into the desert to find solitude and in the silence commune with God. Paul of Thebes is considered to be the first hermit to wander off into the desert, but it was Anthony the Great during Diocletian's persecution of Christians in AD 303 who avoided martyrdom and began the asceticism that came to be known as the Desert Fathers. Several groups came to be formed along the Nile in Upper and Lower Egypt.

I first learned of these men, and sometimes women, from my grandmother, Natalie, who emigrated from Russia in 1909. I wrote about her encounter with Rasputin, in my book, *The Dwelling Place of Wonder*. She also told me about the *staretz*, so-called spiritual advisors in the Russian Orthodox Church. As a young girl growing up in Tsaritsyn, a city that later became Stalingrad and now Volgograd, she was a Protestant, but heard many stories from her Orthodox friends. The *staretz* were wise, old men who lived in seclusion outside the city. People would bring them food and other gifts in return for spiritual advice and guidance in their personal lives. On very rare occasions they might be seen in the city, but mostly they kept to themselves.

Catherine de Hueck Doherty, who was born in Nizhny Novgorod, north of Tsaritsyn, and a contemporary of Natalie, wrote about the *poustinia*, a Russian word which means "desert," just like "hermit" and "eremite" are derived from the Greek word for "desert." While some *staretz* could be *poustiniks* living outside the town in isolation, a *poustinia* could also

The Mysticism of Ordinary and Extraordinary Experience

be a place in the home set aside for prayer and meditation. (My other grandmother, Angelina Serio, had her own room where she would pray her rosary.)

Catherine was the founder of Madonna House Apostolate in Combermere, Ontario. Here, Christian men and women, clergy and lay, dedicate themselves to a life of poverty, subsisting on donations of food, goods and money. They spend their time in prayer, but also in service to the physically and spiritually impoverished of the community. Madonna House has expanded to eighteen houses in six countries.

A reason for this social withdrawal was so that the hermit, anchorite, ascetic could contemplate the presence of God and be filled with the essence of God's love. There is the familiar story of the Zen master who was pouring tea for his student. He picked up a cup that was already filled and kept pouring until the tea spilled over on to the floor. The student said, "Master, you are spilling the tea." The Zen master said, "Observe, you cannot contain what you have no room for. You must be empty in order to receive."

And so the desert fathers of the early church were so named because they went out to the desert to rid themselves of the baggage of living, to get rid of the old habits, the old ways of doing things, old thoughts. This is called "kenosis," an emptying, a ridding of the past—past sins, past guilt, past failures, and being receptive to the new, to the grace of God.

When we consider the life of Jesus of Nazareth, who was very much aware of the presence of God within him, we note that Jesus cultivated those times of kenosis, recognizing God's presence, and being aware of who he was and what his mission was. We could say that Jesus was a "Zen poustinik."

So many times when Jesus sought direction and guidance, when he was overwhelmed by the demands of the crowds, or when he sought affirmation for the tough decisions that he had to make, he went off by himself, or with a few close friends. These times apart were often in wilderness and desert areas, mountaintops, in a boat on a lake, or in a quiet garden. The Apostle Paul says that "though he was in the form of God, he did not regard equality with God as something to be exploited, but emptied himself." (Phil 2:6–7).

Kenosis was not uncommon in the minds of the Jews. After they were led out of Egypt, the Hebrews spent forty years in the wilderness. The number forty is recorded almost 150 times in the Bible. It represented an indefinite period of kenosis, testing, and preparation for what was to come. The forty-year sojourn in the Sinai was necessary for the purging of the memories of Egypt and to become receptive to new ways of living under the law.

American Poustinia

Jesus spent time in his own wilderness to question the voice within him, Satan, that tempted him to abandon the mission to which God was calling him. He had to get rid of the temptations of materialism, fame, and power before he could begin to accomplish the reason for his being. Toward the end of his ministry as he was facing Roman justice and execution, Jesus spent some time apart in Gethsemane wrestling with the issue of abandoning what God was calling him to do. "My Father, if it is possible, let this cup pass from me; yet not what I want but what you want" (Matt 26:39).

The broken heart, the suffering heart, is the heart that is open. One must go through the deep waters, through the valley of the shadow, through the dark night of the soul. Dante Alighieri concludes the first part of The Divine Comedy, "The Inferno," or the journey through hell, with these words: "*E quindi uscimmo a riveder le stelle*" ("And so we emerged and once again beheld the stars.") It is the spirit of God in each of us that binds together all of us on our common journey through life. We will emerge.

Americans living through the coronavirus crisis in 2020 were asked to shelter in place, to maintain appropriate distances from one another, and to avoid large gatherings. For many, it was a time to retreat to a private place, to raise questions about one's reason for living, and God's design for the universe. In a sense, it is our wilderness experience, our *poustinia*, our time of kenosis. As the Black Death transformed European civilization centuries ago, we emerge from our present crises a different people living in a different world. And hopefully, we have a better awareness of the presence of God among us and within us.

Dasein

IN THE COURSE OF a lifetime we encounter many people. Most are strangers who will forever remain strangers. Many others we are introduced to by friends and acquaintances, and after acknowledging each other's presence, we move on. There are some with whom we have extended conversations during a brief encounter and our lives are changed forever because a window in the mind was open to a new idea or a new way of perceiving life. There are those who leave us wishing we had more time to explore new thoughts, new concepts, new perspectives. And there are those who cause us to wish we could revisit those times when we were influenced and shaped by the persons and ideas of those we would meet in later years.

Allen Ginsberg was one of these people. Allen was born in the Weequahic section of Newark, New Jersey, which was more than eighty percent Jewish at the time. Philip Roth, whom my Uncle Emilio knew, was a contemporary and graduated from Weequahic High School. He was another that I wish I could have spent some time with. Though I lived in the nearby Ironbound section, I was born in Beth Israel Hospital, had many Jewish friends, and received a scholarship from B'Nai B'rith which I used to further my theological education. Ginsberg had moved to Patterson, briefly attended Montclair State College before going to Columbia University. He became friends with Jack Kerouac and other Beat poets. It was during these early years that Ginsberg was very much involved in social protest movements. He was anti-war, anti-sexist, and several other antis. Because his mother was an avowed Communist, at one of the trials for his counter-culturalism, he was accused of seeking to overthrow the government, which he vehemently denied. I was familiar with Ginsberg in those early years as I, too, eventually became involved the anti-war, civil rights, and environmental movements.

I also found some affinity with Ginsberg with regard to his mysticism and philosophical leanings. Two of his favorite poets were William Blake and Walt Whitman. Allen said that he had had an auditory hallucination of Blake reading "Ah, Sunflower."

> Ah Sun-flower! weary of time,
> Who countest the steps of the Sun:
> Seeking after that sweet golden clime
> Where the travellers journey is done.
> Where the Youth pined away with desire,
> And the pale Virgin shrouded in snow:
> Arise from their graves and aspire,
> Where my Sun-flower wishes to go.

Ginsberg went on to write his own sunflower poem in which he attributes consciousness to the flower. He later developed the idea that all things are interconnected, that all is one. Though he was raised as a Jew, Ginsberg turned East and began to study Buddhist thought and philosophy, met with the Dalai Lama, and even endowed a Krishna temple. Allen became friends with the Academy Award-winning composer, Philip Glass, who is vice-president of Tibet House in New York. Philip, who had been performing concerts at my church—St. John's United Church of Christ in Kutztown—every four years to benefit the New Arts Program, brought Allen with him one year, just a few years before his death. As we talked briefly in my study, before Philip's concert and Allen's reading, I learned about Allen's concept of a universal state of existence, the practice of mindfulness, and his vision of harmony among all people.

The German philosopher, Georg Wilhelm Friedrich Hegel, was influenced, among others, by the mystic, Jacob Boehme, who contributed much to the spiritual formation of many of the Pennsylvania Germans. Hegel believed that one's awareness of one's existence or being was what made a person who he was. He used the German word, *dasein*, meaning "presence" and was based on the ability to think. The soul consisted of the integration of body and mind, unlike the Greek concept of the separation of body and mind.

Whereas Hegel used *dasein* to mean the state of one's existence, it was the later German professor, Martin Heidegger, who understood *da sein* as "being there" (da—there, *sein*—being). For Heidegger, *dasein* was not a

The Mysticism of Ordinary and Extraordinary Experience

noun, but a verb. It was a person's *modus operandi*. A person is defined by what he does rather than who he is. How a person functions in life says who he is. This then leads to the nature of one's purpose for existing. This ontological distinction then gives meaning to the existence of the entire universe. As each person exists in order to fulfill his or her own purpose, collectively we are all part of God's design and intention for Creation. Heidegger's first academic book, *Being and Time*, describes his concept of *Dasein*.

It is interesting to note that Martin Heidegger became a member of the Nazi party and much has been written about his antisemitism. He believed that the Holocaust was self-inflicted by the Jews. This seems like a rather absurd concept, but according to Heidegger's larger view, this self-annihilation was part of the function of existence. Evil has a purpose in the totality of being. You might say it serves as a learning experience for God. While I am uncomfortable with this philosophy, it does raise questions of ontology and theodicy. It's not over until it's over.

Dasein in the age of coronavirus has taken on a new meaning. How can we be present to one another while practicing "social distancing?" Are video-conferencing and Zoom meetings bringing us closer together? We have gone from the ancient system of communication by means of written letters to a century and a half ago when telephones introduced the age of technology. We now have videophones, Skype, and Zoom. The next stage of development will be the hologram projector. Star Trek's holodeck as a future office and conference center, school room, and worship space now seems plausible. But how can we be there for one another? How do we perfect the electronic hug?

George Orwell's prognostication of a dystopian world in his novel, *Nineteen Eighty-Four*, written in 1949, describes a world of ubiquitous surveillance, loss of individual identity and a totalitarian culture of contradictions presided over by a false messiah named Big Brother who supposedly cares for his workers. Some critics have declared that we have arrived at 1984 in our present time with social distancing, an uncaring leadership, a constant stream of false and misleading statements, and a predilection for re-writing history to accommodate control. There is also the creation of a new form of "Thought Police" who monitor the media for any indication of subversive statements that can be construed as counter to the current political agenda. In this world, the individual is losing his heart, mind, and soul.

Of course, we see the world through our own lenses, our own perspectives and distortions. In preaching my sermon on a Sunday morning, I have as many sermons as there are persons in the pews. Each person comes with his or her own agenda; they hear what they are conditioned to hear or what they feel they need to hear. In the same way, when I lead film discussions at the local cinema, I sometimes wonder if we were all seeing the same movie. We bring to our viewing who we are, our personal history and experiences, our education and social conditioning. It is the way we monitor the world.

There was a thought-provoking Peter Seller's movie called "Being There." Sellers plays Chance, an uneducated gardener at a large estate. He has no identity, no birth certificate, driver's license, medical insurance, and can neither read nor write. One day, by accident, he meets Eve who asks him his name. He says, "I am Chance, the gardener." Eve hears, "I am Chauncey Gardiner." And then follows a series of misunderstandings and distortions that eventually leads to Chance becoming an advisor to the President. His simple statements and observations are taken as profound analyses of the world around him. He becomes the intellectual expert, not because he is, but because we believe him to be. We create other persons according to our own perceptions of them, however accurate or misguided they may be.

The name of the film, "Being There," is that Chance is in the right place at the right time with the right people present. Circumstances affect who he becomes. However, this is no accident. There are no coincidences. What seems to be the result of misperception and misunderstanding may have far-reaching consequences. There is intentionality to the universe, and we are all part of the design. The universe is unfolding as it should. We must be mindful of that, be present to each moment, be aware of who we are and what we are for.

Breath of God

Lobsang Samden, a brother of the Dalai Lama, was a fellow student at Ursinus College in the early sixties. A few of us would gather in his residence at Studio Cottage where he would lead us in some rudimentary form of Vipassana yoga. It was somewhat foreign to me, but I understood and appreciated the meditative and quieting aspects. Lobsang stressed concentration on breathing, and I was to learn how essential this was to seeing clearly what I was about. I had been studying for an exam in abnormal psychology and it was difficult to focus on anything else. Dr. George Tyson, head of the psychology department who taught the course, was very fond of repeating his mantra, "The price of mental health is facing reality." He said that so often that one of his students made a rubber stamp with the quotation and stamped it all over campus, from light switches to napkins in the dining hall. Facing reality took concentration and often the best way of facing reality was not to think about it. That is why Lobsang said that in meditation it is best to focus on one's breathing.

Kundalini was another form of yoga that came from India. I had never heard of it until I attended a lecture by Gopi Krishna in 1979 at the Ben Franklin Hotel in Philadelphia. Krishna is often credited with popularizing this form of yoga in the United States. His lecture on "Kundalini: The Mystery of the Coiled Serpent" also stressed the importance of deep breathing. One's breath is the means of arousing the coiled serpent from its sleep at the base of the spine. Kundalini is the life force or divine energy that lies dormant in the first chakra and the purpose of this form of yoga is that through breathing and awareness, the serpent or energy rises through to the seventh chakra at the crown of one's head. The breathing exercise stimulates the awareness of one's psycho-physical-spiritual persona.

Breath of God

While I have not seriously engaged in yoga, my church in Kutztown had three different classes each week taught by June DeTurk, who at age ninety-five, was still conducting classes in Hatha yoga. Hatha yoga stresses body positions and the very important pranayama (or breathing) that cleanses the entire body and life force. My personal preference was for tai chi and qigong, and we held classes for these and other forms of balancing one's life energy.

Breath is life, and it is the awareness of life. In the Sufi Islamic tradition *zikr* is the ritual litany of remembering God with every breath one takes. As discussed earlier, breath was the essential force of life in Egyptian and Hebrew thought, as well as in other contemporary religions. To focus on the breath is to focus on life and to be aware of life. As with the Sufis, the breath helps one remember the spirit of God within. To give up the spirit is to die. The King James Version of the Bible says that at the crucifixion, "And when Jesus had cried with a loud voice, he said, Father, into thy hands I commend my spirit: and having said thus, he gave up the ghost" (Luke 23:46). The spirit—*pneuma*, ghost, breath—returns to God.

Breathing is being present to the moment. It is being aware of one's surroundings. It is thinking, and it is not thinking. It is simply being.

There is an old story of Zenno who was aspiring to be a Zen Master. After ten years of study, he went to visit his professor. It was a rainy day, so after he arrived on the porch, he took off his sandals and set down his umbrella. When he entered the house, the Master asked him if he had left his sandals and umbrella on the porch.

"Yes," replied Zenno.

"So tell me, said the Master, "Did you leave your umbrella to the left or to the right of your sandals?"

Realizing that he was not being present to the moment and unaware of his actions, Zenno continued another ten years of study.

It is important to understand that the umbrella is the Buddhist symbol for the EightFold Path on how to live the enlightened life.

Mindfulness, awareness, being present is the path to enlightenment. Thus, when Allen Ginsberg entered the ashram and was told, "No writing. No Thinking. Just Be," he was being asked to put aside any cognitive brain function and just be aware of the moment.

When I was in eighth grade, I had a teacher who must have been a Zen Master. He was always saying to his students, "Pay attention." Of course, he wanted us to focus on the subject he was teaching rather than looking out the window or daydreaming about other places we would rather be. I later had a friend who talked frequently about "mind over matter." He would say, "If you don't mind, it doesn't matter." There are things that we must give our full attention to in order to survive and function in this physical life, but there are times when we need to care for our souls and be aware of the presence of God in us.

Edwin Hatch (1835–1889) was an Oxford scholar who wrote a few hymns. His one enduring hymn, "Breathe On Me, Breath of God," refers to John 20:21–22, "Jesus said to them again, 'Peace be with you. As the Father has sent me, so I send you.' When he had said this, he breathed on them and said to them, 'Receive the Holy Spirit.'" The Spirit of God dwells within us.

> Breathe on me, Breath of God,
> fill me with life anew,
> that I may love what Thou dost love,
> and do what Thou wouldst do.
>
> Breathe on me, Breath of God,
> until my heart is pure,
> until with Thee I will one will,
> to do and to endure.
>
> Breathe on me, Breath of God,
> so shall I never die,
> but live with Thee the perfect life
> of Thine eternity.

Prior the battle of Edgehill in the English Civil War, the Royalist commander, Sir Jacob Astley, offered the prayer: "O Lord! thou knowest how busy I must be this day: if I forget thee, do not thou forget me." We are not always able to practice the presence of God as Brother Lawrence would have us do, but to know within our soul that God is with us as we engage in the struggles of life is enough to help us endure and prevail.

Room of Contemplation

I WOULD OFTEN SEE my Italian grandmother sit in the darkened front room of her house on Garrison Street. The half-light of the afternoon sun oozing at the edges of the Venetian blinds was enough to distinguish her presence amidst the shadows. She held in her hands the beads of her faith, fingering them one at a time and whispering the traditional prayers, the "Aves" and the "Our Father." Her lips moved as her fingers moved, but the thoughts that crossed her mind were often not the words that passed her lips.

Angelina was a big woman who expanded horizontally rather than vertically. It was hard to imagine her as the tiny child her mother had named "Little Angel." But her heart was big, and big hearts can be fragile and easily broken. She had buried two of her nine children and her husband, and she worried about the others.

She often sat in the front room which served no other purpose than the formal entertaining of guests, which were few. It was too small for the furniture that occupied it. During the Christmas season only a table-top tree and a papier-maché crèche were accommodated.

But it was a very special room. For my grandmother, it was the room of contemplation. For me, it was the room where she dispensed the quarters and half-dollars to her grandchildren. It wasn't exactly bribery, but it was a way of ensuring the frequent visits of those she loved.

It was the room of her faith. Throughout the house there were crucifixes on the walls, a statue of the Blessed Mother on her dresser, and the Holy Child with a crown on his head. But here in this room was the picture that frightened me the most. It was called the "Sacred Heart of Jesus," but it looked like Jesus having open-heart surgery. With flames coming out of his heart, it could have been an antacid commercial for heartburn. I never understood what it meant, but the sight of an exposed heart was unsettling.

The Mysticism of Ordinary and Extraordinary Experience

Growing up with my other Protestant grandmother I was taught to be wary of "statue-worshippers" and people that used a lot of unusual movements in their worship and at other times. All these rituals like crossing oneself when stepping up to the plate in baseball or running into each Catholic church to put holy water on your forehead or genuflecting before entering a pew—they all seemed like magic. But it was magic that seldom worked. The kids that made the sign of the cross didn't always get a hit, and the holy water was too warm and too little on a hot summer day.

The pictures and rituals, however, did make you feel that a place was actually special or holy. The front room with the open-heart Jesus is where Angelina was present to God. She used the Rosary which she prayed for seven decades to become aware of God's presence. The words held a meaning beyond their meaning. They were an encounter with God on another level of consciousness. She spoke the words, "Hail Mary, full of grace. The Lord is with thee. Blessed art thou amongst women, and blessed is the fruit of thy womb, Jesus. Holy Mary, Mother of God, pray for us sinners, now and at the hour of our death. Amen." She could have been speaking them in Italian or in Latin. It didn't matter. It was more of a mantra than a prayer, much like the Hindus or the dervishes using words accompanied by rhythmic movements. The intention was to achieve the mystic moment. God was in that room. It was holy space. And when she gave me that quarter, it was receiving the grace of God.

Communion, however, took place in the basement. Like so many of the homes in the "down-neck" section of Newark where large Italian, German, Polish, Irish and other immigrant families settled, the houses were not big enough. And so they expanded to the cellars that became the kitchens and gathering places for family and friends. The eucharist served in this kitchen went to the original meaning of the word, that of gratitude for each other's presence. While Angelina must have been Italy's worst cook, and her daughters defensively prepared the meals, Angelina presided. Her words, "Mange, mange," were sacramental, the "Take and eat" of a divine liturgy.

In Roman Catholic tradition, Christ is present in the bread and the wine. Indeed, Christ is the bread and the wine. But in my Protestant tradition, Christ is present in those who receive the symbols of God's love in the bread and the wine. And that's how I saw communion at the Serio table.

God was not in the food (which sometimes seemed to originate in another place); God was in the love that was shared around that table. The true sense of family could be heard in the laughter and in the sharing of stories and the concern brothers and sisters had for each other. Perhaps to outsiders it didn't always seem that way (some of the words meant in jest could be biting, impoverished attempts to be funny or witty), but always there was a love that bound the family together.

In the Breaking of Bread

WHEN MY UNCLE NICK died, my uncles and aunts and cousins were remembering family stories of years ago, and how we would gather around my grandmother's kitchen table. The table was more than a place of nourishment for the body; here we fed our souls. We shared in each other's lives, the joys and heartaches, the laughter and tears. No matter what had happened outside the family, here you were accepted and supported. There was love at this table, and we all knew it.

The film, *Antwone Fisher*, opens with a dream sequence. Based on a true story, Antwone is a sailor who harbors a deep-seated anger and is prone to violent expressions of temper. As a child, he had been abandoned by his mother. In his dream, Antwone as a child is welcomed to a dinner table by all the members of his family, past and present. They receive him warmly with smiles and abundant food. It was an expression of a psychological need to be accepted and to belong.

Apparently, this is a theme that runs through several films where the central focus is a dinner of reconciliation and acceptance. We can cite *Soul Food*, where a fragmented family is reunited because one person takes the initiative to prepare a Sunday dinner. Or *Babette's Feast* where a meal becomes a sacrificial offering of healing. And of course, *Places in the Heart* where the final communion scene brings together all the townspeople, black and white, rich and poor, the powerful and the powerless, the victims and their killers.

The Table Prepared is the eternal symbol of joy, inclusion, welcome, and thanksgiving. It was a symbol for many cultures. In Greek mythology, the heroes who lived well and died well would go to the Elysian Fields where they would dine on nectar and ambrosia, the food of the gods. In the religion of the Norsemen, Vikings who died in battle would be taken by

In the Breaking of Bread

the Valkyrie to the halls of Valhalla where they would spend eternity dining and drinking mead and telling stories. Passover is a meal of remembrance of deliverance and liberation. The first Thanksgiving was meal of gratitude for survival and for the grace of God represented by the harvest. The Holy Eucharist is a symbolic meal of thanksgiving for God's salvation. When a restaurateur opens his kitchen to the homeless, the poor, and the marginalized, it is a ritual of love and caring and kindness to strangers. In all cultures the table prepared brings people together in acts of reconciliation, forgiveness, and gratitude.

If you get up with the sun in Jerusalem and walk the streets of the old city, you will see the shopkeepers rolling back their doors and getting ready for the mix of Arabs, Jews, tourists, pilgrims, and others who will crowd the bazaars. But you will also see young boys balancing trays of freshly baked bread en route to stores and homes. On these trays and on the backs of donkeys are the round pitta bread that serve as both dish and food scoop as well as sandwich bread; there is the chewy sesame bread very much like our soft pretzels and a variety of other kinds of rye and wheat breads. Since these boys seem to be all over the city, I thought they might have been employed by some central bakery, but I found out otherwise.

One evening, while I was working for Hebrew University on the City of David archaeological project, a newly arrived friend who had lived in Jerusalem four years earlier invited me and some of my Jewish friends from Brooklyn to join him as he renewed some acquaintances among the Arabs. We made our way through the dark streets of the Muslim Quarter to a cellar where there was a large oven. Surrounding the oven were chairs, and several men seated there were engaged in conversation. I was told that there were quite a few of these large ovens operated by individuals who do all of the community's baking for both families and shops. These bakeries were also gathering places for conversation and socializing while you waited for your bread to be baked, much as women once gathered at the Laundromat and waited for their clothes to dry. The difference is that in Jerusalem it is the Arab men who gather late into the night. While our conversation was somewhat limited by our need for interpretation, here we were, Christians, Jews, and Muslims, breaking freshly made bread and drinking tea. It was a sacramental act that recognized that we are all children of the same God and have more in common than that which divides us.

Seeing the bread in the shops and carried about the city and visiting the bakery reminded me that to the people of the Middle East, bread was

The Mysticism of Ordinary and Extraordinary Experience

sacred. It was the staff of life—the essential life substance. The story of Moses in the wilderness was shared by both Muslim and Jew. The holy manna, the bread of heaven was given by God to save the lives of the Hebrews. Bread was life itself. To break bread with another was a holy act, as significant as passing the peace pipe was to the Native Americans.

To eat bread with an enemy was a sign of reconciliation. When a refugee was given asylum and broke bread in a house, his host was responsible to defend his guest even at the cost of his own life. Interestingly, the town of Bethlehem, "Bet Lechem," means "House of Bread."

Bread was a sacred symbol of a covenant of trust and mutual responsibility among people. In Christianity there is the belief of a Messianic Banquet to which everyone will have a place at the table. Even Judas Iscariot, who betrayed Jesus, would be welcomed at the Lord's Table. In his poem, "The Ballad of Judas Iscariot," the poet Robert Buchanan imagines the soul of Judas doomed to roam the earth in desolation before seeing the light of the Bridegroom at the door, and hears the voice of Jesus: "The Holy Supper is spread within, And the many candles shine, And I have waited long for thee Before I poured the wine!"

Sharing a meal together can be a moment of mystical transcendence, of the awareness of cosmic hospitality and a God who accepts all.

One without a Name

IN ARTHUR MILLER'S PLAY, "Death of a Salesman," Biff, standing at the grave of his father, says, "He had the wrong dreams. All, all wrong . . . He never knew who he was" (Requiem).

For a man to live a lifetime and miss the most crucial discovery of all—who he is—is the very essence of tragedy. No doubt the phenomenal public reception of this drama in 1949, a time in the post-war years when America was searching for a new identity, was due to the fact that many saw something of themselves reflected in its tragic central figure, Willy Loman, of whom his son exclaimed so wistfully, "He never knew who he was."

We are not born persons, we become persons. We are on a pilgrimage through life to learn who we are and what we are for. We have said that a mystic is one who is aware of the presence of God. The mystic not only sees the God out there in a cosmic void, but an indwelling spirit who speaks to one's consciousness in the gentle voice that is most often without sound. It is a voice that prompts one to love.

It is not enough to know who we are; we must also know who others are. Several years ago, I received a phone call from a funeral director informing me that Edwina Fisher had died. He wasn't certain there were any relatives. For years she had lived alone in her small house outside of town. When I asked one of the elders of the church if he knew anything about Edwina Fisher, I learned that some church women had called on her years back, but no one seemed to know much about her and no one seemed to have cared. The only persons at her funeral were a farmer's family who she had once taught in a one-room schoolhouse. Evidently, she was one of the world's forgotten souls—a woman without a name. Blessed with families, a loving mate, children, and friends who frequently phone, correspond, or drop by, we find it difficult to comprehend the haunting loneliness that is the lot of so many persons.

The Mysticism of Ordinary and Extraordinary Experience

In such a lonely world, in such an impersonal society, the true mystic not only lives in isolation, but becomes the presence of God to other people. To know you as a person is to know you as an end and not as a means. There are many people in our lives who are nameless, but their sheer presence and seemingly insignificant acts can affect us in such ways as to make a difference to who we are. It is the accumulation of the insignificant from persons without names that can shape our destiny.

A member of my congregation spent her life sharing the essence of who she is. Betty Shide made the presence of God alive to other people. She let them know that they are important and valued, that their name was remembered by the community of faith, in the life of the church, and in the heart of God.

For many years Betty not only worked as a volunteer in several community agencies, but her visits to the sick and shut-in, to persons in the hospital, to the almost-forgotten residents of nursing homes had assured them of their connection to the larger body of Christ. In truth, Betty had been the Christ to others. Many did not know who she was and remained a nameless angel, but her visits and her inordinate kindness became the presence of God in their lives.

In her last years, Betty began to lose her memory as the result of dementia. I would visit with her in the nursing home, and as the months passed her recollection of who I was had diminished. In my last visit, before she was able to realize that her pastor was there, she said, "I love you."

How very typical of a woman who loved so much that she gave her life in service to others. Her mental abilities were fading even as her body curled within the warmth of her blanket. She was no longer who she had been, but her soul still reflected the essence of her being. Her mind was gone, but her heart still said, "I love you."

Willie Loman never found the right dreams. He never knew who he was, who he was intended to be. Even his name, "Loman," "LOW MAN," characterized his failure to rise to God's intention for his life. He was a man with no name, no identity, no purpose. And yet, he made a difference.

And so the writer of the letter to the Ephesians admonishes us: "Be careful then how you live, not as unwise people but as wise, making the most of the time, because the days are evil. So do not be foolish, but understand what the will of the Lord is" (Eph 5:15–17).

One without a Name

The mystic, like Betty and like Jesus, is one who has a name and is known because we see God's love in their lives and because we are connected to them because of that love.

Objects

As I watch the television reports of raging wild fires destroy the California mansions of the wealthy and the homes of those who were just trying to get by, my heart breaks for those who must sift through the burning rubble to salvage what they can of their lives. People say it is only things that go up in flames and that material objects can be replaced. But things are often more than things. Like the Ark of the Covenant or the Holy Grail or the relics in churches that attract countless pilgrims or the contents of museums throughout the world that are displayed, objects can have meaning that touch our very souls.

We infuse certain objects with a part of ourselves. They become repositories of memory and can help us recollect meaningful moments in our lives, in our family history, in the history of our nation and of our culture. They can remind us of who we are.

Like so many homes that have been occupied for years by persons who have lived long, traveled widely, and experienced much, my home has its accumulation of souvenirs, artifacts, gifts, and mementoes. To the casual visitor they appear no more than the detritus of living, meaningless knick-knacks that gather dust on the shelves.

My house is no different. Among the more than eight thousand books scattered through several rooms and in boxes stored in the basement and garage, is a large assortment of objects, each with its own tale and memory: the head of Greek hoplite from a visit to Athens; Tibetan *tsingas*, a gift from Ben Iobst who guided my congregation in meditation using prayer bowls; a red Pyrex flask from General Aniline and Film where Mary Ann worked in the lab; an inlaid wood box when I visited family in Sorrento. To any visitor they are meaningless, and most likely will be relegated to the trash or garage sale years from now.

Objects

When I visited Nevin Luckenbill, a retired schoolteacher in his eighties, I commented on the large collection of Hummel salt and pepper shakers that lined the shelves in his dining room. There was a long pause while his mind gathered the memories from his extraordinary past. He taught German and Latin in the local high school and directed the band for many years. When he was a young man, he had received a scholarship from Ferdinand Thun, a local Reading industrialist, to study in Berlin. It was in the thirties, and he had witnessed the beginning of the Third Reich and Hitler's rise to power. While sitting *Unter den Linden,* he saw a parade of Nazi troops and tanks and armored cars demonstrating the power and might of the regime, giving little indication of the terror that was to come. He had bought some of the Hummel figures in Berlin to give to his wife. She later began her collection. Whenever he looked at the shaker sets, his reverie would take him back to his wife, to Germany, and to other times.

When my grandmother, Natalie Wertz, arrived in this country in 1910, she had with her several hundred Russian rubles. They aren't worth much today, but they are beautifully engraved with a portrait of Catherine the Great. As a child, I would hold one bank note in my hands and think of all the hands that might have held this artifact of Imperial Russia. It would conjure memories that weren't mine and I would see people that I had never known. Was it a child's fantasy that imagined a world long ago and far away? Or was there something in the paper money itself that elicited its own fragmented story? It now rests in a case mounted on my wall along with other mementoes of my family's past.

This may have been the beginning of my exploration into the paranormal art of psychometry. Psychometry (from the Greek meaning to measure the *psyche* or soul) believes that any object, especially one long associated with a particular person, can be infused with the essence of that person. For example, a woman's wedding ring or an old man's pocket watch may retain a part of the energy and story associated with the person. The theory may have some connection with the theological belief in "panentheism" in which the spirit of God is present in all Creation, even in the earth itself and in inanimate objects. It may also be related to quantum theory that maintains that the entire universe is vibrational. What appears as a solid object, when reduced to its atomic and subatomic particles, is simply energy in motion. Living beings, natural substances, and fabricated objects all are the coalescence of energy of varying density, and as such, are surrounded by energy fields, creating an aura around persons and things. These energy

The Mysticism of Ordinary and Extraordinary Experience

fields appropriate that which is associated with them. Thus, the theory maintains, a woman's necklace frequently worn over many years, retains the essence and meaning of that person's life.

In many cultures throughout the world, there is the belief that natural objects and places absorb the memories of the people associated with it. In Celtic tradition, the natural world contains the presence of God. The Celts were able to discern the Creator in the works of creation, as one sees the artist in his or her art. Natural objects stored the energies and essences of their surroundings. Oak trees in particular were sacred to the religion of the Celtic tribes for they were the repository of tribal wisdom. The memory of trees retained all that was precious to their existence. To destroy a sacred oak was to cut the heart out of the people who infused it with their life energy. It was to them what they wanted it to be. The Irish singer Enya's album, "The Memory of Trees," does not refer to her own recollection so much as it does to trees as the retainers of memory.

If one recognizes that the presence of God is pervasive throughout the universe and abides not only in living creatures, but is also present in every atom and molecule, then God must exist in the material world. We may need to rethink the so-called sin of idolatry, not only of the ancient peoples who created images of the gods they worshipped, but also of modern religions that make use of venerated statues, images, and other objects. Can there be a distinction between the physical object and the divine presence within that object, and is it solely in the mind of the beholder?

When Ulrich Zwingli visited Rome, he observed the decadence of the church, of prelates living in grand palaces and feasting on lavish meals while the starving poor were begging in the streets. He contrasted the magnificence of the Renaissance churches with the poverty of the masses and declared that the beautiful paintings, mosaics, and stained-glass windows were a distraction from the worship of God. And they were. Instead of using the objects to become aware of the presence of God, they served to reinforce the hedonistic pleasure of providing delight to the senses.

Renaissance artists placed objects in their paintings as hidden symbols to point to both subtle and overt meanings that lead the beholder to additional and sometimes contradictory interpretations. Whether it's the fallen salt shaker in DaVinci's "Last Supper" or the likeness of the human brain in the head of God in Michelangelo's "Separation of Light from Darkness" in the Sistine Chapel, these symbolic objects create a link from the mind of the creator to the mind of the beholder to a universe that encompasses all.

Objects

The objects in my home are not necessarily religious symbols, but they have meaning. Sometimes they conjure the distant memories of people, places, and events that are important to me, and sometimes they are transcendent and point me to new insights and revelations, but always I become aware of the presence of God in my life. I guess my mysticism is different from that of Zwingli.

Emmanuel

IT IS OFTEN SAID that when God seems most absent, that is when God draws closest to us. To be aware of God's presence in times of great tragedy helps us endure the worst that other humans can inflict upon us. Human history in every corner of our planet has its tales of terrorism, genocide, and horrific examples of inhumanity.

While the pastor of a church in Pennsylvania, my congregation was very sensitive to the plight of refugees fleeing from the ravages of war and systematic killing in the Balkans, the Middle East, and Africa.

Emmanuel Niyomugabo and his family had just been released from Berks County Prison where they had been detained for four months following their escape from Rwanda. They came to America seeking political asylum and were now preparing for a new life in this country.

The Niyomugabo family—Emmanuel, his wife, Gaudiose Rutesi, and children, Ivan and Aubine—were briefly the houseguests of Archie and Gini, members of my congregation at St. John's United Church of Christ in Kutztown, before moving on to join Emmanuel's brother, Joseph, in New England. They came to St. John's for worship and the service of healing on a Sunday in September. Emmanuel, who speaks French and Rwandese, but very little English, asked if he could sing a song in his language to show his gratitude to God and to this country for granting him sanctuary. At my invitation, the entire family came forward for the laying on of hands and blessing.

In Rwanda, Emmanuel had operated a soft drink distributorship. He was not involved in politics, but his brother, Joseph, was president of the General Assembly, a position that led to the presidency of the country. Rwanda had constantly been in turmoil as the Hutu and Tutsi peoples contended with each other for political power, culminating in the genocide of

Emmanuel

more than a million persons. Joseph and his family faced certain death at the hands of militarized assassination squads.

Emmanuel helped his brother and his family escape the war-ravaged land by way of Uganda and Canada. He was caught, interrogated, and put into a cell, denying that he had been involved in smuggling his brother out of the country. He was released, placed under surveillance, and arrested again, during which time he was subjected to numerous beatings resulting in broken ribs and other fractures and scars on his arms. Eventually, he managed to get his family out by paying $1200 for visas to Cuba, but coming instead to the United States by way of Uganda and Belgium.

He said that in his country people will go to church and be nice to each other, but when worship is over, the fighting resumes. His photographs showed him sitting in front of a pile of bones that almost reach his six-foot height and filled the entire photo. On his lap he held his father's skull. Another series of photos showed caskets with the lids open. Emmanuel would say "This is my brother. This is my other brother. This is also my brother." The caskets only held parts of bodies.

When Gini saw the photos that Emmanuel showed her while in her home, she couldn't believe what she was seeing. Gini turned on another lamp to see more clearly. Emmanuel observed her stunned silence. She turned the page to wedding pictures. He said, "They are all dead." He had a picture with a view from the front of a full church with all the pews packed with families. He said, "These are all my sisters and their children. They are not living." Apparently, he was among the last of his family to leave the country. Emmanuel does have a sister married to a Hutu, and he says he will send for his two living nieces, nine and eleven years old at the time, who were with his wife's family. Yet, he seemed so willing to smile, to set limits for his kids, to be a good parent, to help in the kitchen, and to be thankful.

Before he left the worship service that day, Emmanuel asked to pray together with the congregation. He expressed his gratitude again and again in English and then said a minute of words in French with his head bowed.

Gini told him to be careful changing buses in New York City. He said he was not worried. In his country people who want to steal will come running up in pairs and pick up the whole person and then they will disappear carrying the person away.

As they sat in the front row on the bus that would take them on the next stage of their new journey, there was the indelible image of them

The Mysticism of Ordinary and Extraordinary Experience

waving from the windows over a freshly painted sign bearing foot-long American flags and the words "Proud to be American."

There are those in this world whose hatred for America is such that they would kill themselves in order to bring this country down. But there are millions more who would risk their lives to attain the political and religious freedom that continues to be a beacon of hope to oppressed people throughout the world.

Dante's words again have particular poignancy. "And so we emerged and once again beheld the stars" (Canto 34). They help me to remember not only Emmanuel and his journey, but also serve as a reminder that life isn't over until it is over, and even then, it is just a new beginning. Emmanuel was named well, for his name means "God with us." And that is what helps us to endure and to emerge.

Mysticism of Jazz

IF I SAID, "IN the beginning God created Jazz," I wouldn't be far off. In the beginning there was sound, the vibration of atoms in a harmonic convergence. Perhaps, it is because we ourselves are sound; the universe is sound. Quantum physics has helped us to understand that sub-atomic particles are merely vibrations of energy—mesons, leptons, electrons—in a continual state of flux. The material world that we think is so solid, when reduced to its atomic structure, is simply energy vibrating at different frequencies. We are sound and when we use such expressions as "resonating to ideas," "feeling bad vibes," "living in harmony," or "getting in tune with," we are using the language of our basic nature and how the universe is structured. It is interesting that even the word *music*, which is the art of arranging sounds, is related to *muse*, "to think creatively."[1]

To the Hindu and Buddhist, one achieves unity with the cosmos through sound. *Nada* is the Sanskrit word for "sound" and Brahma is one of the three personifications of God. The expression "Nada Brahma" means "sound is God" and "God is sound." This concept influenced the music of Ravi Shankar and Philip Glass, who have used a form of jazz to induce a kind of cosmic consciousness. Philip has periodically given concerts at the church where I was pastor, and his music has always been transformative and meditative.

In my childhood years, my relationship with jazz was somewhat tenuous. I grew up in post-war Newark, New Jersey. A large migration of African Americans from the South had come to Newark after the First World War, and a second influx occurred after the Second World War. They came looking for work in the industrial north. They brought with them the music of

---

1. You may want to take a look at Joachim-Ernst Berendt's book, *The World Is Sound: Nada Brahma—Music and the Landscape of Consciousness*.

The Mysticism of Ordinary and Extraordinary Experience

jazz and blues, and there were many jazz clubs in the city. Though she was a little before my time, I went to the same high school, East Side, as Sarah Vaughn. Sarah later transferred to Arts High, the first magnet school in the country specializing in the visual and performing arts. Whitney Houston was also a product of that culture. I spoke with the great jazz saxophonist Kirk Whalum a month after her funeral. Kirk played sax for her, and he said that there was such a massive outpouring of love for Whitney that a six-block area around the church had to be closed. It was also in nearby Englewood that John Coltrane recorded his great composition, "A Love Supreme."

I never became a jazz musician, but a love for the music was ingrained. I became a member of the Berks Arts Council in Reading, Pennsylvania, and in my first year became a founding member of the Berks Jazz Fest, which has become an international ten-day festival with more than a hundred concerts in forty venues, attended by some 40,000 people. It adds some $5 million to the economy of one of the country's poorest city. I have been a part of that festival for all of its thirty years, serving seven years as festival chairman. People have come from all over the country, Europe, and Africa to listen to some of the greatest jazz musicians in the world. Many of these are people for whom music in general, and jazz in particular, is religion. It is that which holds their lives together, which is the definition of "religion." Jazz has become the essence of their lives. Most of us have something that moves our spirits and stirs our souls.

When Bible translators modernized the King James Version of the Bible, they changed the word "soul" to "life" in two-thirds of the cases. Soul is the vitality of the person, the energy that is given by God. Soul is that essence that seeks to return to the Creator. Gaining soul is doing that which makes you feel most alive.

When I'm not watching the performers at the Berks Jazz Fest, I'm watching the audience and observing the effect that the music has on them. In the best moments there is a very visible expression of pure joy and resonance, as though the sound has penetrated every cell of their bodies and consciousness. One does not only hear the music, one feels it. That is why music is so essential to a worshiping congregation that wants to give itself entirely to God.

One of my memorable moments was standing in the wings fifteen feet from Dave Brubeck as he played, "Take Five." That was in 2011. Dave died in December of the following year. For those of us on the stage, it was like the transfiguration, as though we were in the presence of majesty.

Mysticism of Jazz

Jazz and religion are both about the restoration of the soul. They are both about feeling alive. And they are both about expressing what is in the heart that reason and words can never do. As Louis Armstrong said, "You blows who you is."

Dee Coulter, author of the book, *The Brain's Timetable for Developing Musical Skills*, says that jazz resonates the brain at the theta level and promotes creativity.[2] Our consciousness has several levels. We are usually in the beta and alpha levels during waking consciousness. Deep sleep occurs at the delta and theta levels, while dreams occur during REM sleep, mostly as the brain transitions to alpha waves. At the theta level there is increased creativity. It helps a person become alive and renewed. She says that the music of Miles Davis, John Coltrane, and John Cage can lift a listener into theta consciousness—the highly creative brainwave state associated with artistic and spiritual insight. The gamma waves help integrate the various levels and are characterized by heightened awareness.

It's hard to imagine the great theologians of the church, the great mystics, the people for whom the spiritual life was so important, sitting down and listening to a jazz group. Can you imagine Martin Luther espousing his great theological statement while a jazz ensemble is playing in the background?

Many of those who attend jazz concerts in a large auditorium, or perhaps even in a small cabaret, probably experienced moments of deep spirituality that have reached down and stirred their souls and moved their spirits to heights of joy and ecstasy. And I am sure that there have been times when it has aroused other emotions as well. Henry Van Dyke, a minister at the beginning of the last century, hated it and said that "jazz was the invention of demons for the torture of imbeciles." I guess we resonate in different ways.

But we should understand the culture from which our theological forebears emerged. I remember my home church in Newark, St. Stephan's Evangelical and Reformed. The organist would play Bach fugues and other classics of the Baroque period. It was music that was precise, orderly, well defined, with established rules, appropriate for a congregation founded by German *braumeisters* who wanted to have their beer at all meetings. They would never think of free-spirited jazz in worship, but they did put on minstrel shows in which the music of Dixie was featured.

---

2. Campbell, *The Mozart Effect*, 194.

The Mysticism of Ordinary and Extraordinary Experience

For the most part, though, the church in the early twentieth century rejected jazz. There were many who agreed with Henry Van Dyke and said that any music associated with the Negro was pernicious, and jazz was especially considered demonic, having black magical powers. One critic said that ragtime and jazz caused an addiction to alcohol and drugs, and that there was "scientific evidence" showing that ragtime would "stagnate the brain cells and wreck the nervous system."[3]

I have been ministering for many years in Berks County, Pennsylvania, whose county seat is Reading. It is the heart of the German Reformed Church where Henry Harbaugh, who composed its anthem, "Jesus I Live to Thee," was once pastor. And yet in the midst of this grandeur of Reformed and Lutheran music, Reading was once considered the "ragtime capital of the world," publishing more ragtime and jazz than Tin Pan Alley. Jazz invites contradictions.

But sometimes jazz has a way of expressing human pain and longing. Charlie Parker once said that "music is your own experience, your thoughts, your wisdom. If you don't live it, it won't come out of your horn." Many of the great masters of jazz, like so many artists and playwrights, produced their best work in their moments of greatest despair.

So where did Jazz come from? It's America's music. It came out of suffering. From the slave memories of West African rhythms came the blues. I once heard some great West African rhythms from Babatunde Lea's Band. I asked Babatunde what part of Africa he was from. He smiled and said "Englewood, New Jersey," where he grew up as Mike Lea. He learned to play his music in the First Baptist Church there, but it was in his soul. He expressed his roots through his music. Those African beats crossed the Atlantic with the slave trade, and in the rural Mississippi Delta region at the beginning of the twentieth century came the blues descended from earlier work shouts and field-hollers and spirituals. Blues is primarily a vocal narrative style featuring solo voice with instrumental accompaniment. Blues has contributed significantly to the development of jazz, rock music, and country and western music.

It is important to understand that blues came out of the experience of slavery as a resistance to the culture of the white man, unlike the spiritual and gospel music which was an appropriation of white religion. One might say that blues are secular spirituals that do not seek so much to provide answers to human suffering as much as to express the experience of it.

---

3. Leonard, *Jazz-Myth and Religion*, 11.

Mysticism of Jazz

James Baldwin wrote a play, *Blues for Mister Charlie*, which is based on the murder of Emmitt Till, a black youth, in Mississippi in 1955. The murderer, a white man, was acquitted by a white jury. Baldwin makes the point that this society of white Christians can kill black people and justify it in terms of their religion. The play takes places in a mythical location with the metaphorical name of Plaguetown. The plague is not only racial hatred, but also our concept of Christianity—not Christianity itself, but how we interpret it and how we use it. Mister Charlie is the black man's name for his white oppressor. Baldwin's play sings the blues for the white man's moral crisis as much as for the black man's frustration and agony. How interesting that plague year of coronavirus in 2020 should coincide with the rise of the Black Lives Matter movement.

Baldwin raises an interesting and tough question: Should a religion be judged on its teachings and principles or on the basis of those who practice it? For two hundred years in the South, it was white Christians who enslaved, who subverted and repressed, who terrorized and murdered, and who believed that they were worthy practitioners of the Christian faith. From our perspective, we would say that expression was an aberration of Christianity, not an example of it.

So, what do the blues have to say about the problem of evil and suffering in the world? Viktor Frankl tried to tell us that if we could understand the reason for suffering, we can somehow endure it. Sometimes, however, understanding does not mitigate pain and the only way out of the suffering is through it. Singing the blues was a strategy of expressing inner turmoil and pain and therefore moving through it. Blues are techniques of survival and expressions of courage. Just as we cannot move from Palm Sunday to Easter without going through Good Friday, we cannot go through life without pain and suffering. What we experience shapes who we are.

When we talk about the spirituality of jazz, we need to recognize that jazz represents who we are as Christians, and it is also an indication of what we ought to be doing as a church. There are various concepts of jazz that work within the nature our church setting. Whenever you talk with jazz musicians you may hear the term "improvisation." "Improvisation" is derived from a Latin word which means "not provided." In other words, it's not written out. Yes, of course jazz artists will have musical notation, but in jazz, you may have that melody, but usually you play off one another.

The Mysticism of Ordinary and Extraordinary Experience

Chick Corea once asked his mentor, Miles Davis, "When are we going to rehearse?" Miles said, "Just play what you hear; you listen and you play what's inside of you." He said, "Don't play what's there; play what's not there."[4]

Jazz has always been an alternative to mainstream culture. The church has always been an alternative to mainstream culture. When it has become the mainstream culture, it often departs from its basic principles. Many of the teachings of Jesus were not consistent with the culture and religion of his day, and he started a new religion. Jazz is innovative, creative, responsive. It comes out of what is in the person. The drummer Billy Higgins said, "Music doesn't come from you. It comes through you."[5] That's why jazz is authentic music. I have often told my church schoolteachers that the curriculum is not nearly as important as who you are. They will see the Christ in you more than in the words you use. Jazz is the same way. It flows from the heart and soul. The psychologist Mihaly Csikszentmihalyi said that "music events flow in organic fashion without our conscious interference."[6] Consciousness and behavior are one. Improvisation is allowing that flow to happen.

We should never allow tradition to get in the way of vision. God is always doing a new thing. At the Berks Jazz Fest, Dave Brubeck played a few snippets from Bach. Brubeck's classical roots were equally evident in a section from his brother Howard's "Dialogues for Jazz Combo and Orchestra," originally written for the New York Philharmonic under Leonard Bernstein. Brubeck prefaced the piece with typical humor. "We're just doing the improvised part," he explained. "Before this came all that damn Philharmonic stuff." Of course, Dave was giving credit to what came before jazz, but unless you want to become a pillar of salt, the future is where we will live.

We know that the content of the gospel has not changed in two millennia, but we must change the packaging for each generation. Improvisation is interpretation—hermeneutics. Jazz musicians don't make "mistakes" the way we generally think of the word. A mistake is an opportunity to move in a new direction, just as we use the word repentance to change direction.

Gil Rendle, formerly a senior consultant with the Alban Institute and an authority on the transitional church, looks at the declining numbers in

---

4. Leonard, *Jazz-Myth and Religion*, 53.
5. Leonard, *Jazz-Myth and Religion*, 41.
6. Csikszentmihalyi, *Flow*, 108–112.

the Mainline Church. He says, "We don't have a problem; we have a situation." It's a situation that requires improvisation and adaptation.

When jazz became more predictable with the swing era of the big bands, bebop became an improvisational movement that grew out of musicians working together, and working off each other and supporting one another. That sounds like church, doesn't it?

At my former church, we tried to create an alternative community. We had former Mennonites, Quakers, Catholics, Baptists, conservative fundamentalists, and even Wiccans. My Christian Education director was raised Jewish. We were different; we were exciting. And as one colleague described it: we were weird. But it was that kind of symbiosis that permitted us to learn from one another and to recognize that we were all on a spiritual journey to explore our own relationship with God. We listened to each other's music and added our own notes. This was hanging out and jamming. The church is not an institution, but a process; it is a work in progress. The journey is the destination.

Jazz is community. In jazz, you not only perform in community, you practice in community. You "hang out" and you learn. In the 1920's, Louis Armstrong in Chicago would get his musicians together and lock the doors of the club, and they would play for themselves, everyone feeling each other's note or chord and blend with each other instead of trying to cut each other. Victor Turner, who wrote about "liminality" or "threshold experiences," coined the term "Communitas." You had to really know one another in order to create the magic. It's like Holy Communion when the mystical presence of Christ in each person binds the community together.

The true artist does not want to be controlled but wants to be free to create as the spirit moves him, because each person must give expression to his or her own spirituality. Jazz is the music of free expression.

As pastor of St. John's United Church of Christ, I noticed that at least ten percent of the membership was either professionally trained in the arts, performing or creating, or teaching. Many more sought ways to release their creativity.

During my ministry, we gave expression to various musical forms: jazz, Dixieland, minimalism, klezmer, mariachi, Celtic, Indonesian gamelan, Russian. We heard the sounds not only of the sax, but the harp, the balalaika, hand bells, and from full orchestras to the single resonance of the Tibetan prayer bowl.

The Mysticism of Ordinary and Extraordinary Experience

We knew that worship was not only verbal, but involved the full expression of the soul, whether through music, dance, the visual and performing arts, or poetry readings (Beat poet Allen Ginsberg read some of his poetry from *Howl*. I was hoping some of our older members weren't there to hear his creative use of the language). Liturgical movement, a Stanislavsky drama group, annual member art exhibits, and a variety of Eastern meditative and healing arts such as tai chi, yoga, jyorei, reiki and so on, were all part of our improvisation, of doing that which the Spirit moved you to do and of having people in the congregation resonate to that kind of expression. Yes, some people walked out when they heard the sound of a different drummer than the one with which they were familiar, but most learned to listen to the varied sounds of the world and to move to that which had meaning for them.

I did my doctoral work on "Mysticism and Ministry" and the Psychology of Consciousness. If I were to do that again, I would have a section on the mysticism of jazz. For many, both artists and audience, jazz is a mystical experience. It is ecstasy, a word that means to stand outside of oneself. One cannot describe jazz; one has to feel it. Louis Armstrong said, "if you have to ask what jazz is, you'll never know." Or Duke Ellington, "It don't mean a thing if you ain't got that swing."

Some of the jazzmen regarded themselves as prophets, transcending this world to bring back heavenly music. Like many of the mystics who tested the frontiers of sanity, there were some like Scott Joplin and Buddy Bolden who ended their days in mental asylums. Parker and the great bebop pianist Bud Powell also spent time there.

I find the music of Philip Glass transcendental. It's not to be analyzed, but simply experienced without thinking. Philip and Allen Ginsberg were in my study before a concert and I asked him why so many Jews had converted to Buddhism. He laughed and said, "We're called Bu-Jews." The reason is that they had given up on a theistic God of mythology and sought a God that can be experienced in meditation, and in Philip's case, through his music. Many of the Beat Generation were Jews who sought Dharma in Zen Buddhism.

Jazz, unlike other forms of music, is not to be analyzed, but experienced, and perhaps through it, find God. Ornette Coleman said, "Jazz shows that God exists."[7]

---

7. Leonard, *Jazz-Myth and Religion*, 49.

Mysticism of Jazz

****

When Teddy Sommer returned to New York from a safari in Africa, he told Charlie Mingus about his adventure. They were deep in the African jungle, camped for the night. In the darkness, distant drums began a relentless throbbing that continued until dawn. The safari members were disturbed, but the native guide reassured them: "Drums good. When drums stop, very bad."

Every night, the drumming continued, and every night the guide reiterated, "Drums good. When drums stop, very bad."

Then, one night the drums suddenly stopped. The guide looked frightened. "When drums stop, very, very bad," he said.

"Why is it bad?" asked a member of the safari.

"Because, when drums stop, bass solo begins!"[8]

To appreciate that story you have to realize that Teddy Sommer was a drummer and Charlie Mingus a bass player. These are the kinds of stories jazz musicians would like to tell about each other while hanging out.

Bela Fleck is one of the musicians I like hanging out with at our Jazz Fest. Bela has been coming to our festival for more than twenty years. He not only plays jazz, but bluegrass, rock, and world music on the banjo. He does not limit himself to any particular genre. He even plays the classics. Have you ever heard Scarlatti, Bach, Beethoven, Paganini, Debussy all played on the banjo? Listen to his album, "Perpetual Motion," sometime. He said this was the most difficult project he had ever worked on. And he did a lot of it between sound checks at his concerts. On one of his visits to our jazz festival, he had a group from South Africa. It wasn't difficult to see how jazz has become the world's music.

Jazz artists like the Berks festival because it gives them an opportunity to see one another and listen to one another in a relaxed atmosphere, and also to learn from one another. What impressed me was the great sense of community that jazz musicians have among themselves. Over the years, I have had the pleasure to talk with people like Dave Brubeck, George Benson, Dionne Warwick, Nancy Wilson, Rick Braun, Ramsey Lewis, and others. They may be on their separate tours all over the world, but they know each other's music, and they speak a common language, and when they come together in a jam, it is "church"—it is the sharing of their souls; it is

---

8. Crow, *Jazz Anecdotes*, 327.

The Mysticism of Ordinary and Extraordinary Experience

prayer; it is praise; it is theological expression without words. And that's the metaphor for today: the church as a jam session.

In religion, God often picks certain individuals to lead you to a particular point, and then someone else comes along to take you to the next step. Joshua took over from Moses. John the Baptist paved the way for Jesus, and the Apostles carried on his ministry. McCoy Tyner, who was a Muslim, regarded Parker and Coltrane as emissaries charged with bringing divine truth to humans. He said, "John and Bird were really like messengers. In other words, God still speaks to man."[9] (And you thought the United Church of Christ coined the phrase, "God is still speaking.")

Jazz artists have their following. We have a special blues venue as part of the Berks Jazz Fest, and we refer to that group as the "Beer and Winnebago" crowd because so many show up with their campers and follow the blues men and women on their tour.

I do a lot of the introductions and usually I ask them how they want to be introduced and what albums they are promoting and so on. I asked Buddy Guy how he wanted to be introduced. He gave me a whole string of expletives to describe him. I said, "Wait a minute," and got the stage manager to do the intro. He smiled because he probably knew I was clergy. The blues crowd kind of reminded me of the followers of Jesus. Jesus associated with coarse Galileans whose vocabulary offended the rich and cultured Pharisees.

Paul F. Berliner in his study of the jazz community has a chapter entitled "Hangin' Out and Jammin': The Jazz Community as an Educational System."[10] He describes the process of learning how to improvise. Young musicians hang out in a jam session and great learning takes place. Individuals share their talents by forming casual apprenticeships. Jam sessions bring together amateurs and professionals to learn from and with one another. The great masters like Dizzy Gillespie liked to teach technique and theory to the young guys. Miles Davis told how, as novices, he and Freddy Davis would challenge one another by tossing a quarter and telling what note it would come down on. Hanging out was a growing experience.

This is how the church was formed in the early days. We learn the faith from one another, from people we respect and who become our mentors and role-models. If you are not the embodiment of the Christ-spirit, you are not going to communicate the faith. To paraphrase Bird Parker, if it's not inside of you, it's not going to come out of you.

---

9. Leonard, *Jazz-Myth and Religion*, 42.
10. Chapter 2 in Berliner, *Thinking in Jazz*.

Mysticism of Jazz

The jazzmen have developed the art of imitation and improvisation, by listening to the music of others, appropriating it, modifying it, taking it to another level, and owning their own style. In the jazz community there is a constant struggle between leading and following, interdependence and individual freedom, the search for that right balance to be able to play freely but within the group. Freedom has limits and responsibilities.

In the church, we call it a covenant relationship, of respecting the spiritual development of each individual as that person seeks to discern how God is speaking to him or her, and yet at the same time being faithful to the gathered community so that collectively we may discern God's will in our communal and societal life. That is especially true in these troubling times when we need to listen to each other and together discern what God is saying to us. There are times when we ought to step to the music which we hear, but there are other times when we need to find the common beat. Somewhere among the volume of voices that support the war in Afghanistan and those that lift their voices for peace, we need to listen for the faint whispers that tell us we are one family and that we need to live together.

Jazz artists know something about being a voice of protest, about criticizing the establishment. In fact, jazz has always functioned as a social alternative to mainstream culture. Our German forebears, when they came to this country, brought with them a love for high classical music—the music of the court, and the church, and later, the concert hall—the ponderous Beethoven symphonies and Bach chorales. They referred to symphonic music as sermons in tones and disdained the "unlaundered Negro and American Indian" themes, the plantation songs of the African slaves, which became the basis for jazz.

The music of the newly liberated slaves evolved from spirituals to early gospel music to ragtime to blues to bop to new jazz which had no rhythmic formulas but stressed its African origins. There are some who attend the jazz fest that are what others call "the jazz police." They talk about "real" jazz or "true" jazz and about a return to the authentic jazz and away from this "smooth jazz." But I'm not so sure what that means, or how far back in the evolution of jazz some people want to go. Maybe somewhere there is an audience for Amish Jazz.

The point is that jazz encourages permutation and change. Nothing is ever static. So, too, the church must be a prophetic voice in a constantly changing world. It must continually speak out for the love of God in new ways and in new forms of expression. Just as bebop became an alternative

The Mysticism of Ordinary and Extraordinary Experience

to swing, the church must show the world that there are other alternatives to bringing peace to our planet.

Jazz has always been the background music for social change, and the history of jazz parallels the transitions in the culture, the economy, the mores, and the way we see each other through the eyes of God.

Billy Strayhorn, who composed "Take the A Train" after Duke Ellington told him how to get to Harlem, was an openly gay man and very much involved in the civil rights movement. He was a friend of Martin Luther King Jr. and in 1963 arranged and conducted a piece called "King fit the Battle of Alabama" for Ellington's orchestra. The great Harlem Renaissance brought changes not only to the arts and entertainment industry, but I believe there were other seeds planted in the Apollo Theater, the Cotton Club, and Small's Paradise that affected the entire country. (Incidentally, Earle Hagen's "Harlem Nocturne," written in 1939 for Duke Ellington, was our unofficial East Side High School class song after the Viscounts recorded it in 1958.)

We are all one family, and we need to focus on that which unites us, not that which divides. We need to focus on the Scripture which says, "For God so loved the world" (John 3:16), and understand that to mean the entire world, and not just our part of it.

The church would do well to adopt the jazzmen's art of hanging out as a model for hanging out in the world, and by jamming they may discover that music that binds us together.

So much of our great art and music has emerged from the crucible of pain. When African and European music first began to merge to create what eventually became the blues, the slaves sang songs filled with words telling of their extreme suffering and privation. One of the many responses to their oppressive environment resulted in the field holler. The field holler gave rise to the spiritual and the blues—notable among all human works of art for their profound despair. They gave voice to the mood of alienation that prevailed in the construction camps of the South, for it was in the Mississippi Delta that blacks were often forcibly conscripted to work on the levee and land-clearing crews, where they were often abused and then tossed aside or worked to death.

When you consider some of the great blues singers and jazz musicians, so many of them died young. When I was in Kansas City for General Synod several years ago, I visited the Phoenix, the club where Charlie Parker played. Parker experienced many personal difficulties throughout his life. Often in debt and addicted to alcohol and drugs, he endured broken marriages, suicide attempts, and imprisonment. His death at the age of thirty-four was the result of a number of ailments, including stomach ulcers, pneumonia, cirrhosis of the liver, and a heart attack. Bird Parker is buried in Kansas City. Parker never wanted to go back to Kansas City, and he certainly didn't want to be buried there. But his mother had other plans.

Billie Holiday, whose mother was only thirteen when she was born, grew up in a brothel. It was there she first heard the music of Louis Armstrong and Bessie Smith on an old Victrola. Billie died at the age of forty-four in New York, almost unrecognizable—thin, drawn, haunted. She had sold off her clothing to feed her habit and her little dog. Even on her deathbed, someone managed to smuggle heroin into her room. Joe Glaser, who paid for her funeral as he had done for Charlie Parker's, said that her death was a concoction of everything she'd done for the last twenty years. Billie's signature song was "God Bless the Child," a song she wrote after an argument she had with her mother over money. The lyrics, "Them that's got shall get, them that don't shall lose, so the Bible says, and it still is news," most likely refers to Matthew 25:29.

Whitney Houston performed the song during her 1997 HBO Concert special, "Classic Whitney Live from Washington, D.C." It was performed as a tribute to Diana Ross who had also sung the song in portraying Billie Holiday in the film, "Lady Sings the Blues." Whitney enjoyed the heights of success, but also experienced the depths of despair.

Ethel Waters was born in Chester, Pennsylvania, as a result of the rape of her teenaged mother, Louise Anderson. She was raised in poverty and never knew the love of a family. She married at the age of thirteen to an abusive husband. Her most familiar songs were "Stormy Weather," and "His Eye Is on the Sparrow," which reflected her beginnings. I heard her sing that song at Billy Graham's New York Crusade in Madison Square Garden in 1957.

"Georgia Tom" Dorsey was the son of a Baptist preacher. His mother was the church organist who told him to stop playing the blues and "serve the Lord." He ignored her and returned to Chicago, playing with Ma Rainey. He married his sweetheart, Nettie Harper. Then, in August, 1932, while performing in St. Louis, he received a telegram saying that his wife had died giving birth to his son, who also died. He returned to Chicago to bury his wife and son in the same casket. In his despair he went to a friend, and

The Mysticism of Ordinary and Extraordinary Experience

then found a piano, and began composing a song, "Precious Lord," that has touched the hearts of all who have heard it.

John Coltrane, whose addictions led to his early death, recovered in time to compose *A Love Supreme*, a synthesis of music and religion to the glory of God. Coltrane said, "My music is the spiritual expression of what I am—my faith, my knowledge, my being . . . When you begin to see the possibilities of music, you desire to do something really good for people, to help humanity free itself from its hang-ups . . . I want to speak to their souls."[11]

Even as music, and especially jazz, comforted these artists in their affliction and perhaps inspired them in their addiction, we know the therapeutic quality of music. Don Campbell explains this in his book, *The Mozart Effect: Tapping the Power of Music to Heal the Body, Strengthen the Mind, and Unlock the Creative Spirit*. Different forms of music have different therapeutic qualities.

When Pablo Casals, the renowned cellist who played in the White House at President Kennedy's invitation, was an old man, almost ninety, he was beset with the infirmities of age, which incapacitated his whole body. But Casals was able to cast off his afflictions, at least temporarily, because he knew he had something to celebrate—his musical gift. His music was an act of praise. This was his daily cortisone for his creaking joints. It is said that Casals would walk into the room stooped over, bent, hunchbacked, in apparent pain. He painfully sat down at the keyboard of the piano which he also knew how to play, and slowly and with great labor, began to press the keys and the pedals, and slowly, the music of a Bach creation began to emerge. The fingers straightened. The spine became more erect, and within two or three bars of the music, Casals was moving up and down the keyboard in a rhythmic frenzy. He finished the piece, got up from the piano, and was good for an hour or two, in a state of relative well-being. Casals filled his painful void with celebration and praise and thereby coped with his condition.

Jazz has helped many artists cope with their afflictions. Pat Martino, a lovely, sensitive guitarist from Philadelphia, had suffered a severe brain aneurysm and underwent surgery after being told that his condition could be terminal. After his operations he could remember almost nothing. He barely recognized his parents and had no memory of his guitar or his career. He remembers feeling as if he had been "dropped cold, empty, neutral,

---

11. Quoted in Porter, *John Coltrane*, 232.

cleansed . . . naked."[12] In the following months, he made a remarkable recovery. Through intensive study of his own historic recordings, and with the help of computer technology, Pat managed to reverse his memory loss and return to form on his instrument. His past recordings eventually became "an old friend, a spiritual experience, and the music itself helped in his recovery."

Sometimes jazz does not result in physical healing. Jeff Golub, a great guitarist who played with Rod Stewart and had his own group, "Avenue Blue," had a collapsed optic nerve and went totally blind. In September, 2012, he fell on the subway tracks in New York and was dragged by a train until he was rescued. When I saw him at one of his last concerts in Reading, he was playing with Henry Butler, a great keyboardist who is also blind. It really was a case of the blind leading the blind. Jeff credits Henry with helping him accept his situation and navigate through a new world. When I introduced Jeff, I said that he might have lost his sight, but he hadn't lost his vision. God's healing is not always of the body, but of the spirit, and God can use the afflicted to teach us what is really important in life. Incidentally, Jeff's final album before his death is called, "Train Keeps a Rolling," a good metaphor for his life and the persistence of the spirit.

While songs and music may express the soul's longing and aspiration, it also expresses the power and majesty of God's presence. Jazz may not be the language that speaks to you. You may find your mystical experience in the written word, or in art, or in the natural world, or in the silence of quiet reflection, or perhaps in human love and relationships. But however God chooses to speak to you, and however you choose to listen to God, the important thing is that you do listen. Especially in those times of doubt and despair. That is when the song will be heard most clearly, and you will find your way through the dark night.

The Apostle Paul says that regardless of what is happening in your life, you must press on, not looking behind to what is past, but rather to the future, knowing full well that there are no accidents in life, but God's intention (Phil 3:12–15). We need to trust the love of God and move on with a song in our heart and music in our soul. In the end love will be the final word. And when the last trumpet is sounded at the close of the age, it will be jazz.

---

12. Martino, *Here and Now*, 1–3.

The Mysticism of Ordinary and Extraordinary Experience

LOVE THAT JAZZ

It was a love affair
  both erratic and erotic.

  She came to me one steamy summer night—
    a child lying in the dark
    waiting for sleep.
  Her sultry voice sifted through the screened window
    and kissed my ear.

  There's something about the sound of a saxophone
    playing soft jazz in the night,
      like all the world is lonely and alone,
      like a train whistle across an open prairie
      that tells you someone is going somewhere,
        but you're not.
  I didn't know her then,
    but I heard her blue voice,
      and I cried.

  We met again in the Village
    —a little basement room on Christopher Street
      with sawdust floors and Chianti candleholders.
  She spoke in progressive rhythms then
    while we sipped espresso and
    talked of Ferlinghetti and Kerouac,
      the search for Dharma and for Zen.
  I fell in love with the beat of her bass
    as she haunted me through Harlem nights
      and sunrises in Washington Square.
  It was my time of innocence—
    a time that never was and never could be,
      even as I lived it.

Mysticism of Jazz

I heard her briefly at the funeral of a friend.
    It was springtime in New Orleans.
       On the way to the cemetery her sweet trumpet voice sang
          "Just a Closer Walk With Thee."
She could have been whispering to me,
    but I would not listen, for I heard a different drummer.
She seemed so old, so much out of time, out of place.

She came to me again last night
    and spoke with another voice,
       young, vibrant, sensuous,
          a swinging beat
              that seduced me once again
              and carried me to new worlds
                  of joy and ecstasy.

—Harry L. Serio

Sexual Mysticism

ONE OF THE MOST popular Christian hymns during the past one hundred years is "In the Garden," written in a cold, dark basement in New Jersey. It became the favorite of the old ladies of the church who fantasized about a love affair with Jesus. Just consider these words:

> I come to the garden alone,
> While the dew is still on the roses . . .
>
> And he walks with me, and He talks with me,
> And he tells me I am His own,
> And the joy we share as we tarry there,
> None other has ever known.
>
> He speaks, and the sound of his voice,
> Is so sweet the birds hush their singing,
> And the melody that he gave to me,
> Within my heart is ringing.
>
> And he walks with me, and he talks with me,
> And he tells me I am his own,
> And the joy we share as we tarry there,
> None other has ever known.

This is sexual mysticism. But it's not unusual in the long history of the church. When nuns were ordained to their orders as consecrated virgins, they became the brides of Christ, sworn to chastity. This may have had precedent in the Vestal Virgins of ancient Rome who tended the sacred flames of the hearth in the temple of Vesta and also took a vow of chastity. Celibacy was designed so as to devote oneself entirely to the love of God.

Sexual Mysticism

However, with so many "brides of Christ," a theological question might be: would that make Christ a polygamist?

Many of the religious orders were based on devotion to and adoration and emulation of the Virgin Mary. But according to the New Testament, Mary didn't remain a virgin, or were Jesus' brothers and sister (Matt 13:43; Mark 31:32) only half-siblings, having a different father (Joseph)? The scriptural evidence, of course, points to the fact that Jesus was born out of wedlock. The church tried to reason its way out of this conundrum by teaching that James, Joseph, Judas, Simon, and the sisters were not "actual" siblings, but they were "brothers and sisters" because of their close association with Jesus. Some church leaders argued that Joseph had been previously married. Anything to maintain the perpetual virginity or sexlessness of Mary.

There arose within the church a theology based upon "bridal mysticism." This theology derived from several references in the gospels and in the writings of Paul. Jesus referred to himself as a bridegroom (Mark 2:19), and Paul in his letter to the Ephesians compares the union of husband and wife to Christ and the church (Eph 5:22–33). John of Patmos speaks of the great wedding banquet at the close of the age with Christ as the bridegroom (Rev 19:7–8).

Many of the medieval mystics actually interpreted some parts of the Old Testament with this bridal imagery in mind. The prophet Hosea was told by God to marry the prostitute Gomer, who, after she gave birth to three children, ran off to practice her harlotry. Nevertheless, Hosea relentlessly pursued his wayward and immoral wife. While this was a metaphor for God's relationship with Israel, some Christian writers maintained that it was analogous to Christ and his sometime profligate bride, the church.

The Song of Solomon with its lusty sexual images was sometimes considered a metaphor for union with Christ and also for Christ's love for the Virgin. The twenty-five lyric poems or canticles contain much sensual and erotic imagery. (While Sunday School teachers encouraged us to read the Bible, they told us to skip over the Canticles because it was not for children. Of course, there were other parts of the Bible that would be considered X-rated).

Origen, in his third century commentary on the Song of Solomon, not only compared it to Christ and the Church, but he also believed that it referred to Christ's relationship with the individual Christian. John, the epistle writer, repeatedly affirms, "God is love" (1 John 4:8). But what sort

The Mysticism of Ordinary and Extraordinary Experience

of love? The Greeks made a distinction between the pure love of the spirit (*agape*) which John consistently uses, and sexual or erotic love (*eros*). There was also the love of friendship (*philios*). Origen didn't see much difference between *agape* and *eros* since both emanated from God. After all, when God said, "be fruitful and multiply" (Gen 1:28), God wasn't talking about arithmetic. Erotic love is derived from God in order to perpetuate the human race and therefore is part of the essence of God.

This no doubt influenced Bernard of Clairvaux who in a series of sermons on the Song of Solomon used much sexual imagery in describing a relationship with Christ. He wasn't attempting to breach the then prevalent vow of chastity as much as he wanted to use the strongest language to illustrate the connection that the devout Christian should have with Christ. The strongest erotic language cannot fully describe the desire of the Christian to love Christ, but Bernard, John of the Cross, and others tried. For Bernard, the kiss represented a desire, a yearning hunger for the sheer joy of Christ's presence.

Hildegard of Bingen, the twelfth century abbess and author of *Scivias* and many other works, often looked upon creation in sexual terms. She wrote about divine fertility and saw the universe as a cosmic egg. Her illuminations are rich in sexual images. She saw women in a somewhat subservient role and had the nuns in her charge dress in bridal attire when they received Holy Communion, which was divine union with Christ.

Rupert of Deutz, another early twelfth century Benedictine theologian and mystic, was so enamored of the imagery in the Song of Solomon that he applied it to the Holy Eucharist. Christ was not only in the bread and wine of the Sacrament, but that the elements were actually the body and blood of Christ. This concept was known as impanation. It differed from that of Transubstantiation where the bread of the sacrament becomes the body of Christ. With impanation, it is Christ that becomes the bread. Rupert was falsely accused of this by the adherents of Consubstantiation, namely followers of Martin Luther who believed that Christ was mixed in with the elements. Nevertheless, Rupert did consider taking the host as French-kissing Christ.[1] Pope Benedict XVI spoke of Rupert's defense of the Eucharist in his weekly catechesis on December 9, 2009 when he cited Rupert's *De Divinis Officiis*.

---

1. "I beheld him, living, in my mind's eye . . . I took hold of he whom my soul loves, I held him, I embraced him, I kissed him lingeringly. I sensed how gratefully he accepted this gesture of love, when between kissing he himself opened his mouth, in order that I kiss more deeply" (cited in Mills, *Suspended Animation*, 177).

Sexual Mysticism

While celibacy and virginity were regarded by many of the early mystics as a means of identifying with and becoming aware of the presence of God, there were some who thought particular lifestyles might be a distraction. Meister Eckhart and others affirmed a knowledge or belief in God that transcended whatever we might do to try to attain such knowledge or belief. Eckhart said that what matters is who we are, not what we do.

We, too, are incarnated spirits. Our embodied selves must recognize that it is more than a vehicle of consciousness, but our means of relating to the world and giving expression to the love of God. We are sexual beings, and in our thoughts, feelings, and actions, we should be aware of the God who created us. To fail to affirm a person because of gender or sexual orientation is to deny the Creator God who is within us.

Folk Spirituality of the Pennsylvania Dutch

AFTER MARTIN LUTHER NAILED his ninety-five theses to the door of the chapel at Wittenberg Castle, which became the flashpoint of the Protestant Reformation, the Roman Catholic church quickly took measures to suppress the heretics who dared to defy the authority of Rome. Thus ensued the wars of religion beginning with the Peasants War, the Schmalkaldic Wars, and many others. The most devastating was the Thirty Years War, concluding with the Peace of Augsburg in 1648. It didn't resolve much except to give recognition to three church entities: the Roman Catholic Church, the Lutheran and the Reformed churches.

Europe was laid waste. Marauding armies pillaged the towns and farms, burned crops, and destroyed civil institutions. Millions died in battle or from famine and disease. Many viewed the events in apocalyptic terms as signs of the end of the world. The four horsemen were riding forth as prophesied in the book of Revelation, and their names were War, Famine, Pestilence, and Death. For the Protestants of the Palatinate (die Pfalz) in southwestern Germany, this was *Lilienzeit*—"*the time of the Lily*"—when Christ would come again, for the lily had been associated with the resurrection of Jesus. They looked forward to the second coming of the Messiah with a "holy longing" (*sehnsucht*), for the time appeared to be fulfilled when Christ would come again.

The Messiah did come, but not in the form that they had expected. He came in the form of an English Quaker named William Penn. Penn had received some land in the new world as payment for a debt that King Charles II of England owed his father. Wanting to colonize this land, known as Penn's Woods, or Pennsylvania, with an industrious people who would settle the land and cause it to prosper, Penn went to Frankfurt in 1677 and began his recruitment of Germans. The first migration was that of Swiss

Folk Spirituality of the Pennsylvania Dutch

Mennonites in 1683 who arrived in Philadelphia and settled in an area that is still called Germantown. More migrations of Germans followed, especially after the War of the League of Augsburg when the Palatinate was virtually annihilated by the forces King Louis XIV of France. Almost one-fourth of the population of the Palatinate emigrated to the new world.

These German settlers also arrived in Philadelphia and moved up the Schuylkill River to around present-day Boyertown and formed the first German Reformed congregation in Pennsylvania under the leadership of John Philip Boehm in 1715. The first Lutheran congregation in Pennsylvania was founded by Henry Melchior Muhlenberg in Trappe. Some German groups moved up the Hudson River and settled in the Schoharie area of New York, but many of these colonists then migrated south in 1723 to the Tulpehocken area of Berks County in Pennsylvania under the influence of Conrad Weiser.

The Reformed and Lutheran congregations, known as the "Church Dutch" after the Peace of Westphalia, and Anabaptist groups, consisting of Mennonites, Brethren, Dunkers, and later, Amish, weren't the only groups to establish communities in Pennsylvania. There were others who engaged in mystical and esoteric practices.

The Germans who settled in eastern Pennsylvania are often called "Pennsylvania Dutch." "Dutch" was an English corruption of the German "*Deutsche*." The Palatinate area of southern Germany from which they emigrated were lands which in Roman times were inhabited by the Celts. While the terms "Gauls" and "Celts" refer to the same people and that most scholars believe that the Celts had their origin in Central Europe, there are some that believe that Celts may have emerged from the Indo-Europeans who migrated over the centuries from Anatolia, the La Tene and Hallstadt cultures of Austria and southern Germany, and eventually to the British Isles. Many of their folk traditions influenced the spirituality of the Allemani, Franks, and other groups who supplanted them in the Palatinate.

The Celts were panentheists who believed that the spirit of God was present in all things, especially living things. Their spiritual leaders, Druids or shamans, communicated with the natural world. They developed the art of natural healing and invoking "God presence" to foster healing. The Celts also consulted animals such as serpents or badgers to predict the weather. Their celebration of seasonal transitions was assimilated into Germanic folk traditions and brought to this country by the settlers of Pennsylvania. Thus, Imbolc on February 2 became a time for weather prognostication

The Mysticism of Ordinary and Extraordinary Experience

known as Groundhog Day. Beltane on May 1 related to Ascension Day (a major celebration of the PA Dutch). Lughnasah on August 1 was the observance of First Harvest and Midsummer Communion. And Samhain on November 1, the approach of winter, became a festival of the dead or Totenfest (All-Saints Day).

Hildegard of Bingen (1098–1179) was a Renaissance woman before the Renaissance. She used the curative powers of natural objects for healing and wrote treatises about natural history and the medicinal uses of plants, animals, trees and stones. She preserved much of the Celtic arts, and her theological writings influenced the mystic Meister Eckhart, as well as Johannes Tauler and Henry Suso, and to a lesser extent, Martin Luther. Luther adopted Celtic pre-Christian symbols—the pine, wreaths, evergreens, candles—and reinterpreted them with Christian meanings.

When I first moved to eastern Berks County where I became pastor of St. John's United Church of Christ, one of the oldest Pennsylvania German congregations in the area founded in 1736, I met John Joseph Stoudt. John was part of our ministerial association. I liked him as a teller of jokes and Dutch stories. I knew him to be a professor and historian, an authority on Pennsylvania German culture, but I didn't realize until his passing how much I would have liked to have learned from him. John was the author of some thirteen books and numerous academic articles, but was most noted for his book about Jacob Boehme (1575–1624), the German mystic who had much influence on the Germans who settled in Pennsylvania.

Boehme stood in the great line of German mystics that descended from Gnostic and Neoplatonic roots. These mystics from the Rhineland, such as Hildegard and Mechthild of Magdeburg, Meister Eckhart, Henry Suso, Johannes Tauler, along with Boehme, contributed to the ideas that laid the foundation of several utopian communities in the new world.

Johannes Kelpius arrived in Germantown, now a part of Philadelphia, and gathered some followers along the Wissahickon Creek in 1694. The group came to be called "The Society of the Woman of the Wilderness" based on Revelation 12:14–17. This cabbalistic group practiced alchemy and built an observatory with a telescope to watch for the Second Coming which they expected in 1770. After Kelpius died in 1708, the group disbanded.

There were other strange groups like the Newborgnen or the New Born in the Oley Valley who believed that they were created before the Fall and therefore were sinless. The New Mooners who settled near Conrad Beissel's group at the Cloisters in Ephrata felt that only prayers offered

Folk Spirituality of the Pennsylvania Dutch

during the new moon would be granted. Beissel, of course, had his own fantastic beliefs such as the hermaphroditic Christ and the austere separation of the sexes. A strict vegan, he administered a diet devoid of meat and dairy, but with plenty of buckwheat and cabbage. Beissel had intentions of joining Kelpius in Philadelphia, but arrived a few years too late and thus established his group further inland in Lancaster County. There were several other semi-monastic groups at places such as Snow Hill and Rose Hill.

Pennsylvania German spirituality was primarily phenomenological, based upon the experience and inner reflection of the worshipper. Prayer is not only the words that are said, but what one does. When a Pennsylvania Dutch artisan illustrates an object with a distelfink or a tulip or a lily, the design is itself a prayer, an expression of love for God emanating from the work one does.

There was also a sort of "revelational transcendental" quality to the spirituality of the Germans living in Pennsylvania. Transcendentalism as espoused by the New England philosophers such as Ralph Waldo Emerson and Henry David Thoreau was panentheistic—it saw divinity in each person and in all things. Individuals would be far better off if left on their own and were not corrupted by society. Even organized religion was a corrupting influence. John Stoudt pointed out that the "full blown rose of mystical transcendentalism blossomed in Pennsylvania a full century before New England's scrawny plant began to bud." For the Pennsylvania German, God was revealed not only in nature, but in daily life and in individual creativity, but what was most important was that the person experienced it. A good resource for further study is *Pennsylvania Dutch Folk Spirituality*, edited by Richard E. Wentz. Professor Wentz was a fellow Ursinus College and Lancaster Theological Seminary alum and established and chaired the Religious Studies Department at Arizona State University. He did extensive research on John W. Nevin and the Mercersburg Movement.

In the new world, folk spiritual practitioners, known as "powwow doctors" or braucherei (meaning "tradition" or "custom") brought their healing arts from the old world. The term "pow-wowing" (from the Algonquin) indicates that many brauchers, since they were unfamiliar with the indigenous pharmacopeia, also learned from Native Americans

The brauchers also functioned to remove hexes and spells in order to protect persons and property. They relied on ancient sources for their wisdom: Albertus Magnus (1193–1280), the Kabbalah, Talmud, Egyptian and other ancient sources. Especially useful were the Sixth and Seventh Books

The Mysticism of Ordinary and Extraordinary Experience

of Moses with their emphasis on the names of God. In 1820, John George Hohman, wrote a manual called *The Long Lost Friend* which contains many of these folk remedies and spells, some of which use sympathetic magic and homeopathy. A famous braucher in the Berks County area was Maria Jung, known as Mountain Mary, who was not only a herbalist, but who presumably used a combination of faith healing, energy healing (a form of reiki, chi, huna), and spiritual intervention.

Hexerei is the opposite of braucherei and used black magic or evil spells. It is falsely believed that barn signs, commonly called hex signs, were used to protect cattle from witches who would poison their milk, but they are really "just for nice" as the natives would say. However, farmers would paint false doors on their barns so that flying witches might crash into them.

In the study of the folk customs of any society, one becomes aware of a universal recognition of a transcendent spiritual realm with which humans have interaction. Whether they are naive superstitions and folk tales passed down from generation to generation or the results of observation and interpretation, it is the nature of the human species to be aware of alternate realms of existence and to seek a wisdom that lies beyond the traditional ways of knowing.

Parataxic Totemization

"Art is the final product in the parataxic totemization of the traumatic aspects of the numinous element," wrote John Curtis Gowan in his privately printed book, *Trance, Art and Creativity* (1975).

We have come a long way in our attempts at defining art or judging what is good art and what is not. There are many who would prefer not to define it at all and simply say, "I know it when I see it!" and "If I like it, it's good art." Like truth and beauty, art can also be a very subjective thing. Gowan is right when he says art is an aspect of the numinous, deriving from the depths of one's own spirituality. Art springs from the mind of its creator and resonates in the mind of its perceiver. When it has established that communicative link, it has fulfilled its function—one mind speaking to another. Parataxic totemization is the action of the mind in creating symbols as art represents the inner workings of creativity. Art can be an entry point to the mystical state.

John Keats, writing about the discovery of a Greek artifact surviving in the dust of two millennia, called it the "still unravished bride of quietness . . . foster child of Silence and slow Time" ("Ode on a Grecian Urn"). Art, like the Grecian Urn itself, often comes from the mind at rest, when one is not thinking about the daily routines of life and the business of making a living. It is the stuff of dreams and daydreams, of fantasy and visions. It is a break from the ordinary, of discovering something uncommon about the mundane. We need those periods of life when time slows and we can think uncommon thoughts. We need those sabbaticals of the soul when our creative juices can flow. We need those times of quietness when we can let art speak to us and inspire us, challenge us and teach us. We need those pauses in life when we can rediscover truth and beauty.

Years ago it was the practice of those who desired to discover their own inner nature and be attuned to their higher self to retreat into the

The Mysticism of Ordinary and Extraordinary Experience

desert and practice what the ancient Greeks called "kenosis"—an emptying of oneself. One needs to unload the baggage of preconceived notions and rigid mindsets, to unlearn what one has been taught. Before a bowl can be filled it must first be emptied. The new world cannot be discovered without leaving the shores of the old. Purgation prepares us to be receptive and to be renewed. This is why we take "vacations"—to vacate the familiar and the routine so that we can have a renewal of mind and spirit.

There are times when life slows down and when each of us can discover the artist and poet within us. Plato once wrote: "The poet is a light and winged and holy thing, and there is no invention in him until he has been inspired and is out of his senses, and his mind is no longer in him; and when he has not attained to this state, he is powerless and unable to utter his oracles" (Ion). Yes, we do need to be out of minds occasionally.

"I don't want realism. I want magic," Blanche tells Mitch in Tennessee Williams' *A Streetcar Named Desire*. "Yes, yes, magic! I try to give that to people. I misrepresent things to them. I don't tell the truth. I tell what ought to be truth. And if that is sinful, then let me be damned for it! Don't turn the light on!" (1.9) In the beginning of Williams' *The Glass Menagerie*, Tom tells the audience, "The play is memory; it is not realistic" (1.1).

We live between reality and fantasy, between memory and hope. And art is the lens that focuses and distorts our perceptions of truth and what ought to be truth. Fantasy helps us see reality, and memory keeps hope alive. The artist, through the creative process, helps us to look at life and see it from a different perspective. That perspective may be through the shared experience of the artist or through the invoking of our own life experiences. Sometimes, through art, we are invited to visit the mind of the creator. Sometimes we may be compelled to wander through the closed rooms of our own minds to reexplore forgotten insights or reexamine old memories and lost truths. On other occasions, we are given a tour of the undiscovered regions of worlds that interface with our own, but which we have largely ignored because we either didn't have the time or the interest or perhaps the courage to give them consideration.

The Film Society of Lincoln Center ran a program in 1994 called "The Ministry of Illusion: German Film 1933–45." It was a program of twenty-nine entertainment films, largely comedy, musicals, historical epics, and melodramas, representing most of the motion picture production of the Third Reich. Tom Reiss, in his *New York Times* review, says that Joseph Goebbels, Minister of Popular Enlightenment and Propaganda, was given the task of creating the Hollywood dream factory in hell. He was operating under the theory that propaganda worked best when an audience didn't know it was there.

Thus, when the real war turned against Germany, the war of illusion was brought in. The cinemas were the first buildings to be reopened after the air raids so that the populace could participate in an alternate reality and not confront a demonic ideology. The danger in politics, as well as in one's own state of mental health, is not recognizing the difference between reality and illusion.

For some reason or another, the holiday season that surrounds the winter solstice always seems to bring with it a collection of cinematic art that takes us on flights of fantasy and illusion. For example, in 1994 we witnessed the season's offerings: *Stargate, Star Trek: Generations, Mary Shelley's Frankenstein, Interview With a Vampire, The Santa Clause*, etc. Every year we resurrect our traditional fantasies such as *The Nutcracker* and *Miracle on 34th Street*.

We need fantasy; we need myth. They help us look at ourselves and see who we really are, where we have come from, and where we are headed. When you watch Charles Dickens' *A Christmas Carol* again, let the three spirits not only conjure the past, present and future, but let them also induce memory, insight, and change.

Don Quixote, the Man of La Mancha, was right: "Too much sanity may be madness and the maddest of all, to see life as it is and not as it should be." We require times for fantasy and for dreaming and for truth. But we also need to know the difference.

The Defenestration of the Soul

WOODY ALLEN WAS ONCE asked if he would sell his soul. "Why not?" he replied. "I'm not using it."

Allen's dream, in which he envisioned the soul as the size of a chickpea, raises the question as to whether the soul has any substance. Does it have mass and volume and weight? In 1907, Duncan McDougal published his research in which he weighed the bodies of some dying persons immediately before and after death and concluded that the difference of 21 grams was the weight of the soul. Given the accuracy of his equipment and several other explanations, his experiments were inconclusive and much criticized.

If a soul, or for that matter a ghost, has mass and weight, it would be subject to the laws of physics and gravity that would keep it earth-bound. The question then arises that if it has substance and physicality, it cannot be considered an apparition. Is the soul, therefore, simply a mental construct, a product of the brain? The scriptures report that the resurrected Jesus materialized in a room and offered Thomas the opportunity to examine his body, prompting the position that Jesus is not a ghost, but a reanimated body that can also eat with the pilgrims on the road to Emmaus or have breakfast on the beach with his disciples.

There have been many reports of the so-called out-of-body experience. Robert Monroe, founder of the Monroe Institute, was a researcher who wrote *Journeys Out of the Body*. Monroe describes his own experiences in which a "second body" goes to distant places and observes what is happening. This second body, he says, has substance, that is, weight, and responds to environmental stimuli, although to a much lesser degree than the physical body. It can sometimes be seen by other persons. It raises the question of how a limited, almost non-physical entity, can observe and hear. What is it that is doing the seeing and hearing?

The Defenestration of the Soul

The English poet William Blake, who was with his beloved brother, Robert, at the time of his death from tuberculosis, described seeing his "released spirit ascend heavenward through the matter-of-fact ceiling, 'clapping its hands for joy.'"[1] Was this the soul of the person, the reason why the Pennsylvania Germans built "soul windows" in their houses so that the released spirit could return to its Creator?

Is the soul simply a theological or philosophical concept whose existence reason demands to explain the human presence in the universe? Or does it have substance that can be verified by empirical analysis?

A book, *The Soul Hypothesis: Investigations into the Existence of the Soul* by Mark C. Baker and Stewart Goetz, probes the borders of physics, neuroscience, psychology, philosophy, and linguistics to find elements of commonality and makes a strong case for a scientific reexamination of the soul's existence. This may be considered soft science since many of the rules of empirical study may not be appropriate. However, consciousness is far more than the neural apparatus that processes it. We may be able to reduce a person's preference for a particular color to a reinforced series of neural pathways in the brain. We may allocate responses to a dangerous situation to the function of the amygdala. We may choose our "soul mate" based upon intellectual and sexual stimulation as well other feelings of pleasure caused by an affinity of like interests, ethnic and cultural similarities, or some obscure desire for personal fulfillment. However, the reduction of the soul to a purely biological or psychological process without consideration of one's reason for being and ultimate destiny does not satisfy our longing to understand the "why" question of our very existence.

Rather than simply tossing the soul out of the window, it should be considered both scientifically and theologically. When the prophet Mohammad was asked, "What is the soul?" he replied that it is what God does. We do not possess a soul; we are a soul. On the Temple of Apollo at Delphi were inscribed the words, "Know thyself." Aeschylus, Socrates, Plato, and others had different interpretations of its meaning, but in truth to really know oneself is to know God and to explore God's intentions for one's life.

Hildegard of Bingen, in one of her many mystical "Illuminations," depicts an unborn child in the mother's womb connected by an umbilical cord to a representation of an all-seeing and all-knowing God. In Michelangelo's painting of the Creation in the Sistine Chapel, God reaches out to Adam, supposedly to bestow the divine spark of life. Their fingers do not

---

1. Gilchrist, *The Life of William Blake*, 60.

The Mysticism of Ordinary and Extraordinary Experience

touch, yet Adam appears to be fully animated. Perhaps the energy crosses a synaptic gap. What is important in both these illustrations, and in many others, is that it is God's action that bestows life, and the soul is the part of God that is infused in each person.

Avatar

Exploring Things Visible and Invisible

I SPENT A WEEK on Cape Cod at a conference on the spiritual aspects of contemporary film. While *Star Wars* and *Avatar* were not part of the general discussion, I was struck by certain similarities and relevance to Paul's letter to the Colossians, as well as themes that relate to the nature of consciousness, reincarnation, and the interconnectedness of all things.

At the beginning of *Star Wars: The Empire Strikes Back*, Luke Skywalker is near death when he sees a vision of Obi-Wan Kenobi who tells him, "Luke, you must return to Dagobah and learn the ways of the Force."

Luke is rescued, and follows Obi-Wan's advice, seeking out the Jedi master, Yoda, to learn the ways of the Force. Eventually, Luke uses his newfound power to save the universe (including his wayward father, Darth Vader) from the clutches of the evil empire.

Star Wars is the great American myth for our era, Homer's *Odyssey* for the space age. In place of gods and monsters that provide divine wisdom and thwart the hero's journey, George Lucas has described a new unseen power from the fourth dimension known as the "Force," an energy field created by all living things. It surrounds us and penetrates us. It binds the galaxy together.

Everyone seems to be looking for the cosmic glue that holds and connects all things together, that binds all people in a common consciousness or spirit. Many religions recognize the presence of the divine in all things and celebrate the interconnectedness of the universe.

Before we dismiss all of this so-called "New Age" thinking about an unknown and mysterious Force that resides in the natural world and holds all things together, we need to be sure that we aren't using different languages in speaking about the same thing.

The Mysticism of Ordinary and Extraordinary Experience

When Paul wrote to the Christians at Colossae, he reminded them of the nature of the avatar Jesus of Nazareth: "He is the image of the invisible God, the firstborn of all creation; for in him all things in heaven and on earth were created, things visible and invisible . . . all things have been created through him and for him. He himself is before all things, and in him all things hold together" (Col 1:15–17).

"Avatar" is a Sanskrit word which means "descent" or "cross over" and refers to the divine becoming manifest in human form, or incarnated (taking on flesh). To that extent, we are all avatars and thus the Hindu greeting "Namaste," which loosely translates, "the divine in me recognizes and honors the divine in you." In the movie, *Avatar*, this is similar to the Na'vi greeting, "I see you," which conveys recognition and engagement.

Avatar combines elements of various spiritualties, such as Celtic, that are panentheistic, i.e., "God in all things," and that all living things have an interconnected consciousness. The magnificent Tree of Souls in the movie is representative of the world of Pandora which is based on the Gaia Principle that the world itself is a living organism. Knowledge comes through shamans who are in touch with the ancestors through the Tree of Souls and the living world, much as the ancient Druids consulted the sacred oaks, which were the repositories of tribal wisdom. We can also compare this to Yggdrasil, the immense tree of Norse mythology where the gods convene and make decisions affecting the nine worlds that surround it.

The conflict in *Avatar* comes when a spirit-filled world faces a world based on materialism and technology. We see a materialistic and militaristic force, a futuristic military-industrial complex, exploit the natural resources of a planet as it suppresses the indigenous population. Ironically, it is technology that is both bane and blessing, for it enables the consciousness of Jake Sully to become incarnated as a Na'vi and thus become their savior. One can therefore use the Taoist argument that good and evil are two sides of the same coin and that the universe is unfolding as it should. Science and the paranormal are two ways of understanding the nature of reality, each seeing only part of the total picture.

In *Star Trek: The Motion Picture* there is an interesting metaphor for the meaning of existence. The crew of the Enterprise encounters a bionic race of aliens that somehow has discovered the American spacecraft Voyager 6 and interpreted its mission as defined in its computer program to *"Learn all that is learnable. Transmit that information back to the Creator."* To accomplish this, the living machine has replicated itself repeatedly to an extraordinary degree and accumulated a vast amount of knowledge. In so doing, it has also developed consciousness. Its mission is to reunite with its Creator which brings its closer to earth and the source of its being.

While Gene Roddenberry considered ideas from sci-fi writers such as Ray Bradbury and Harlan Ellison, the mysticism of *Star Trek* has its roots in the heart of the human quest to know and to unite with that which brought all existence into being. It is as though humans have a built-in homing device to merge with their Creator and to report all its accumulated knowledge and experiences.

There are some philosophies and religions that claim that God is the accumulated consciousness of all living entities and that the totality of the human experience resides in the mind or consciousness of God. This concept goes beyond Carl Jung's "concept of the collective unconscious" in which shared archetypes, primordial images, instincts, and other archaic vestiges reside within the entirety of the species.

With this newly gained consciousness, V'ger, the spacecraft Voyager with some letters blackened out, wants to see the Creator and learn if there is nothing more to its existence than seeking information and bringing it back to the Creator. The story is an allegory of humanity's search for God and the knowledge of who God is. However, when V'ger first comes into contact with the *Enterprise*, V'ger refuses to accept humans as "true life forms," to which First Officer Willard Decker replies: "We all create God in our own image."

Perhaps Pseudo-Dionysius the Areopagite was on to something when he asserted that we can only know God by describing what God is not. And going a step further, the anonymous author of *The Cloud of Unknowing* suggests that if you are looking for the Creator, don't bother. God is hidden deep within you, and it is there you might find the divine essence of all that is.

Movies not only reflect culture, but helps culture confront the great issues and ideas of our times. There is a growing awareness that we are indeed spirits who have a body rather than bodies that have a spirit. *Avatar, Star Wars, Star Trek* and other films not only illustrate this growing consciousness, but they raise some interesting questions about our nature and our destiny and our search for the Creator.

Walkers between Worlds

The Celtic Mystic Tradition in a Postmodern Age

IN THE PAST QUARTER-CENTURY there has been a resurgence of interest in things Celtic. From Thomas Cahill's best-seller, *How the Irish Saved Civilization*, to the music of Enya and the Chieftains to Riverdance, Irish is in. The spirituality, philosophy, and "New Age" sections of many bookstores feature books by John Philip Newell, Caitlin Matthews, John O'Donohue, Nigel Pennick, Nora Chadwick, and many others. Tales from Celtic mythology and folklore are being retold in new forms, and ancient characters have shifted their shapes and are morphing into or influencing new beings from Tolkien to George Lucas. Even Darth Vader has been given a Celtic realm over which to preside. He is known as the "Dark Lord of the Sith," which resembles the Celtic word *sidhe* in its spelling. The *sidhe* are fairies who are known as beings of light and renowned for their great beauty. More about *sidhe* and the banshee (*bean sidhe*) later on.

To help us understand the Celtic mystic tradition and its impact on our postmodern age, we must consider the Celts, who they are and where they came from, their religion and its assimilation into Christianity and their influence on German mysticism and the Pennsylvania Germans in the New World, the Celtic spiritual tradition and the importance of the "thin places." The thin places are locations where the veil between the physical world and spiritual world is particularly thin so as to enable enlightened persons to walk between worlds.

Today there are six areas in which the inhabitants can claim a Celtic origin: Ireland, Scotland, Wales, Cornwall, Isle of Man, and Brittany. Of course, almost every European can have a legitimate reason for celebrating St. Patrick's Day since the Celts moved from one end of Europe to the other over a thousand-year journey and left their mark upon the land and the cultures that would follow them.

The origins of the Celts are uncertain. There is some evidence that leads scholars to believe that they may have had their beginnings in northern India and then migrated to Anatolia. The Galatians, to whom the apostle Paul addressed an epistle, were a Celtic people, and you can see the common root of names like "Gael," "Gaul," and "Galatia." A dominant settlement was established at Hallstatt (c. 700–500 BC), which was based in the area around Upper Austria and Bavaria. By the sixth century BC, Greek authors wrote of a people called the 'keltoi' in southern France and at La Tene in Switzerland (450–100 BC). Keltoi is not quite the same as barbaroi (barbarians), but seems to have meant something like "the other" or "stranger." They never referred to themselves by this Greek term, but used tribal names which appear in Caesar's *Commentaries on the Gallic Wars*, names such as Belgi, Veneti, and so on. Herodotus located them in the region around the Danube. In time, their settlements stretched from Turkey and the Balkans right across to western Europe. At the peak of their power, they were strong enough to sack both Rome (386 BC) and Delphi (279 BC). The memory of these victories was soon eclipsed, however, by the rise of the Roman Empire. Here, the lack of cohesion between the various Celtic tribes proved fatal. One by one, they were overrun or expelled from their territories. Eventually, they were pushed back to the western fringes of the continent and then the migrations to the islands of Britannia and Hibernia where they found a home.

Excavations at Hallstadt and La Tene revealed a distinctive Celtic art style using swirling curves and geometric shapes in abstract designs. Animal and human forms are stylized, unlike Greek and Roman art with its emphasis on realism. Celtic art was not just a poor attempt to copy Greek art, but showed the Celts had an entirely different way of looking at the world.

The Celts believed in an immortal soul, and that death was the passage into the "Otherworld," a world parallel and similar to this one. After a time in the Otherworld, a person would be reborn into this one, and so the cycle would continue. The concept of reincarnation was part of Celtic theology. It is interesting to note the proximity of the Celtic center at La Tene to the Albigensian stronghold in the south of France where a thousand years later this people were persecuted as heretics and their belief in reincarnation condemned.

The Mysticism of Ordinary and Extraordinary Experience

Also known as Cathars, this group followed a form of Manichaeism and Gnosticism, which many of the Celtic tribes had adopted. They also recognized the feminine principle in religion and the preachers and teachers of Cathar congregations were of both sexes. At the same time, the Cathars rejected the orthodox Catholic Church and denied the validity of all clerical hierarchies, all official and ordained intercessors between man and God. At the core of this position lay a gnostic tenet—the repudiation of "faith," at least as the Church insisted on it. In the place of "faith" accepted at secondhand, the Cathars insisted on direct and personal knowledge, a religious or mystical experience apprehended at firsthand. These are practices that can be traced to early Celtic religion and the Druids.[1]

Druids were a special caste of nobles, both men and women. They acted as judges, priests and bards. Bards were like a living library, who would orally recite knowledge of history, science, and laws. The Celts were not illiterate and used Greek letters for writing, but believed such knowledge was too important to write down where anyone could read it. They also feared that such knowledge would have a harmful effect on the people. The Celts believed that wisdom resided in the earth, that trees and rocks and streams, as well as animals, retained a memory of what was important to the tribe. However, because of the changing shape of the landscape and migrations, and other forms of disconnection from the sources of wisdom, the ancestors of the tribe would also be summoned for guidance and encouragement. The Druids were able to make this contact with the ancient wisdom. In fact, the name Druid derives from two words meaning "oak tree" and "wisdom." The correct translation, therefore, would be "wisdom of the oak" or more generally speaking, "wisdom of nature."

The Druids were priests and healers, but they were also the connection between the physical and spiritual worlds. They probed the mysteries of the unseen, the world beyond this world.

The Druids were familiar with the natural pharmacopeia and recognized that healing emanates from the earth since humans are creatures of the earth and have a connection to rocks and trees and animals. There is an energy latent in the natural world. When that arch-Druid, Obi-Wan Kenobi, says that there is a "disturbance in the force," he may have been saying that there is a distortion of creation, a distortion in the way God intended things to be. Christians would call this sin. The created order was meant to be a unity, a common mind or energy. The Druids provided that

---

1. See Guirdham, *The Cathars and Reincarnation*.

priestly function as mediators between worlds and thus as healers of the created order.

The early Celtic religions were based on the worship of nature. They saw God in the natural world, in rocks and trees, in animals and flowers. This world was filled with spirits, elves, fairies, leprechauns, and other creatures who inhabit the middle earth between the familiar and the magical, between our physical dimension and the spiritual realm. This is the realm of the Sidhe, the so-called "Good People," beings of light. This belief was once common throughout all the Celtic countries, in localized forms. The Sidhe are considered to be a distinct race, quite separate from human beings, yet who have had much contact with mortals over the centuries. It was believed that this race of beings had powers beyond those of men to move quickly through the air and change their shape. They once played a huge part in the lives of people living in rural Ireland and Scotland.

It was the *Bean Sidhe* (woman of the hills), a spirit or fairy who announced a death by wailing or keening. She would visit a household and by wailing she would warn them that a member of their family was about to die. The *Bean Sidhe* has long streaming hair and is dressed in a gray cloak over a green dress. Her eyes are fiery red from constant weeping. When multiple Banshees wail together, it will herald the death of someone very great or holy.

The religious leaders of the Celts were called *file* (fee-lyee), Irish Gaelic for "vision-poets." These were persons who were able to see beyond this world into the spiritual world. They could contact the Sidhe.

Shamans were certain individuals who were chosen because of their ability to interpret the spirit realms. "Their task is to explore these unseen realms by means of the spirit-journey, . . . to interact with beings they encounter there and to retrieve knowledge, healing and advice which may benefit the people."[2]

The Celtic shamans were believed to have the power of shapeshifting, to morph into any living creature in Middle Earth or in the Otherworld. This ability to polymorph is similar to the mystic's union with all creation. While the mystic doesn't seek to assume any form but his own, the Celtic shaman may shift shape because the human form is a disadvantage, its energy alignment being unsuited for the spiritual realm. One might compare this to the so-called "astral body" or to the Apostle Paul's discussion of the spiritual body. The reason for the shamanic shapeshifting might be for

---

2. Matthews and Matthews, *Encyclopedia of Celtic Wisdom*, 1.

The Mysticism of Ordinary and Extraordinary Experience

several reasons: to learn from animal guises, to hide by becoming invisible, to survive in dangerous places, or to protect someone. The lorica, or verbal breastplate, was used to protect the shaman on his spiritual journey. As with many other Celtic ways, Patrick and others adapted them to Christian use, and the Christian *lorica* called upon the powers of the Trinity and the elements of creation to protect a person in a perilous age.

The Celtic shamans were the gifted people or *aes dana* who could walk between worlds with ease—the Druids, poets, and seers. After the adoption of Christianity, the shamanic skills of the *filidh* and *aes dana* were assumed by the clergy, became more formalized, and were practiced less. A few individuals and families retained this knowledge as their direct heritage.

The concept of the "walker between worlds" was not unknown in the Roman culture. The high priest of the Romans was known as *"pontifex maximus,"* the chief bridge-builder, the one who enables access to the gods. The title was later assumed by the pope, who is often called pontiff, from pontifex, the maker of bridges, in this case the mediator between human and divine.

Edward Sellner, the author of many books and articles on Celtic spirituality identifies eight characteristics of the Celtic spiritual expression as it was adopted into Christian practices:[3]

Of primary importance is a sense of love, awe, and wonder of the natural creation in which the presence of God is most evident. They were panentheists, seeing God in all things. Celtic Christians often refer to God as "Lord of the Elements" and experience communion with God in their natural surroundings. This deep respect for the environment is manifested in a quiet care for all living things. There is a sense of wholeness to the created order. There is a similarity here to ancient Greek mythology that saw spirits, gods and goddesses inhabiting rocks, trees, streams, and other natural places.

A second characteristic of Celtic Christianity is a love for learning. Commitment of the mind to the study of Holy Scriptures and expanding one's knowledge of God and God's world is prized as worthy and honorable work. Thomas Cahill in his book, *How the Irish Saved Civilization*, attributes this to the monks who labored in the scriptoriums preserving ancient manuscripts.

A third characteristic is an innate yearning to explore the unknown. The theme of pilgrimage is one of the key elements of Celtic spirituality. To

---

3. Sellner, "Celtic Spirituality and Prayer, 4–9.

make a spiritual journey for Christ—despite the hardships—brings blessings, increased intimacy with God, and the healing of the body and the soul. The voyages of St. Brendan the Navigator are indicative of this wanderlust.

A fourth characteristic is the love of solitude and isolation. Solitary places and times of silence are valued and encouraged for reflection and spiritual shelter. Many of the Celtic spiritual centers, such as Iona and Lindisfarne, were remote islands.

The Old Testament prophets regarded God's words and actions as affecting all time, not just the specific situations of their day. The Celtic tradition lived more in *kairos* time rather than *chronos* time. *Kairos* time is time that has meaning and fulfillment, and is relative to the past, present, and future. An event occurs when it is ripe for it to occur, not when an artificial calendar says that it should occur. It's not that the Celts didn't recognize special days or seasons. They did. And they had special days to mark the light part of the calendar and the dark part.

Mentioned earlier were the Pennsylvania Germans appropriation of the Celtic observances to mark the passage of seasons: Imbolc, Beltane, Lughnasadh, and Samhain.

Beltane, May 1, was the first day of the light part of the year, when cattle were driven through bonfires to protect them and ensure fertility. So, too, young couples would dash through the fire to obtain this fertility. Lughnasadh, August 1, was the beginning of harvest and the celebration of the god Lugh who sacrificed for the sake of humans and hung from a tree. Of course, Lugh was similar to Christ and the holiday became a Christian observation but was too similar to Easter to survive in the Christian calendar.

A sixth characteristic is an appreciation of ordinary life. The ordinary daily routine is valued. The Celts believed in the eternal now. The Kingdom of Heaven is a present reality as well as a future hope. God is found not so much at the end of time when the reign of Christ finally comes, but now, where the reign is already being lived in God's faithful people. God is worshiped in daily work and in very ordinary chores. This is the mysticism of ordinary experience which Brother Lawrence described in his little book, *The Practice of the Presence of God*. Even in washing the dishes one can feel the power and presence of the divine.

A seventh characteristic is the Celtic belief in the great value of relationships, especially the spiritual ties of special Christian brothers and sisters called "soul friends"—the *anamchara*. Each person should have a

The Mysticism of Ordinary and Extraordinary Experience

spiritual mentor or guide—a soul friend who offers a compassionate ear or a challenging word. God speaks to us, heart to heart, through our friends. Sometimes the *anamchara* is not only a spiritual guide, but a spirit guide who accompanies us unseen through life and helps us interpret the meaning of what is happening to us.

A final characteristic brings together much of the others. Like many other cultures, particularly the Jews, the Celts had their share of suffering and pain. Whether it was the Potato Famine of the nineteenth century or "the Troubles" of Irish rebellion in the early twentieth century, and other afflictions, Celtic people learned to deal with loss. The Irish wake is legendary. It was a social gathering where the deeds of the deceased were retold, often with humor, and put in the context of the entire familial structure, I found it interesting when in Ireland and meeting new friends at the local pub, my travelling companions with Celtic names were not asked what they did for a living as is common in the United States. They were asked who their family was and how were they connected. The Irish wake was a time for memory, for healing the broken fabric of the deceased's connection to the family and to society.

The wake was held in the home and is derived from "the watch" or prayer vigil offered for the soul of the dead. There may be a connection to the ancient Hebrew custom of *shimira*, the guarding of the body prior to burial, not only to protect it from vermin, but to give comfort to the lost and confused soul of the deceased which was believed to hover over the body until final burial.

The aforementioned Thomas Cahill says that the Irish monks who were just learning how to read and write themselves when Rome was being sacked by the barbarian tribes, copied everything they could get their hands on. They became the saviors of western civilization, the narrow conduit by which the ancient world was able to flow into the medieval world. If it hadn't been for this forgotten role in history, there would be no western civilization as we know it. When Mahatma Gandhi was asked what he thought of western civilization, he was reported to have answered, "I think it would be a good idea." Thanks to the Irish and their brief moment on the world stage, we would have none of the ancient writings, including much of our scripture, that have influenced the modern era. The Celts were "walkers between worlds" in this cultural sense as well.

Each year at my church we have a Celtic service celebrating an aspect of Celtic spirituality, using music by the *Shanachians*, a ceili group, and occasionally with step-dancers. There are some who still believe that this is an anomaly in a Pennsylvania Dutch culture, but I try to impress upon them that much of their folk spirituality and even some of their German mystical traditions derive from the time that the Celts inhabited the areas of southern Germany from which many of the Pennsylvania German forebears emigrated. We are indeed all part of the same human family and connected in many ways.

When the Celts were driven out of Europe by the Romans, the Allemani descended from the north and settled in southern Germany. The Allemani were influenced by the Celts but were of a different ethnicity. Centuries later along the Rhine a group of women mystics began to reclaim much of the Celtic lore and wisdom. These were people such as Mechthild of Magdeburg and Hildegard of Bingen. Hildegard was a true renaissance woman three centuries before it flowered in Germany. She was an artist, musician, healer, mystic, theologian, philosopher, and church leader who established an abbey at Bingen. The "Brother Cadfael" stories on PBS were patterned after her.

Hildegard's writings influenced many of the German mystics such as Johannes Tauler, Henry Suso and Meister Eckhardt, who in turn influenced Martin Luther. Luther's followers as well as the spiritual descendants of John Calvin and Ulrich Zwingli came to Pennsylvania where they mixed the Celtic wisdom passed on through Hildegard with the wisdom gained from Native Americans to develop their own Pennsylvania Dutch spirituality. This includes the healing arts using natural herbs along with certain rituals as performed by the *braucherei* or "pow-wow" doctors, the latter-day Druids. It included the use of incantations and spells as found in John George Hohman's book, *Pow-Wows, or Long Lost Friend*. They also believed in revelational transcendentalism and looked forward to a time when they would be able to transcend this earth and walk between worlds. Several of these esoteric and mystical groups sprung up in the wilderness in the early 1800s.

Officially, the church did not have much use for Celtic spirituality. They embraced it in order to win converts but tried to suppress many elements of its mystical nature. While many modern Celtic lands such as Ireland and Brittany are Catholic, Scotland, Wales, and Cornwall are predominantly Protestant. Catholic Christianity emphasized the meaning of ritual and wisdom passed on through tradition. Protestant Christianity emphasized education and reason so one could interpret the inherited wisdom. Both were dependent on other humans for the means of accessing the divine.

The Mysticism of Ordinary and Extraordinary Experience

The Celtic mystical tradition emphasized the direct knowledge of God through the natural world and through the gathered community. Mysticism is the unification with the One or some other principle; the immediate consciousness of God; or the direct experience of religious truth.

While Celtic spirituality has provided much of the paranormal esoterica, we must not forget that there is also a rich tradition that is quite relevant to our postmodern age. We are living in a time when definitions are subject to negotiation. When Bill Clinton tried to parse his way out of his testimony by saying "it all depends on what your meaning of 'is' is," he was representing the essence of postmodernism. There are no absolutes; truth is defined by its context. How you see and interpret the world may be different from how I see and interpret the world. What may be a UFO to you, may be a vision to me, or swamp gas to someone else. Postmodernism does not have a worldview. It has replaced knowledge with interpretation.

The Celtic mystical tradition provides a lens by which we can see and interpret reality. It is not the only lens, nor is it necessarily a valid one. It is just one filter that can help us make sense of our experiences and understand who we are and why we are. It gives us a perspective so we can find meaning in our existence.

Entering the Cloud of Unknowing

FATHER FRANCIS DIGEORGIO AT Mount Carmel Church in Newark was my favorite priest. If I were a Roman Catholic, I would attend Mass every Sunday just to be in his presence. You felt a genuine love emanating from him. His soft-spoken words and gentle eyes immediately signaled that he was someone who took an interest in you. When he asked how you were doing, he really wanted to know. Because of Father DiGeorgio, I learned that it was not important to understand the words or ritual of the Mass, but to be in the church when he was celebrating was to be in the presence of holiness. When he died, it was as though a light had gone out in the religious experience of the world.

After too many conferences, too many words, I get to the point of apophasis where words no longer express feelings or thoughts, where you kind of transcend the moment, and the spiritual exercises offered by the leaders seem contrived and artificial. There are times in prayer when I don't want to say anything or hear anything or see anything. I just want to be and experience the love of God without having to describe it.

I walked to my car after attending a meeting in the city. The meeting had concluded with the leader having a short worship of scripture, "words of inspiration," prayer, and blessing—words, words, words. As I made my way to the parking lot, I looked at the people around me—some talking on cell phones, some waiting for the traffic light to change, some disgusted with themselves or with their lives, some dreamily facing their futures with hope and confidence, some so much in love that nothing else seemed to matter, some spewing anger and hate. No, I couldn't tell for sure, but each face seemed to reveal that which was occupying his or her heart and mind.

Suddenly I was overwhelmed with the thought that all the billions of people on this planet had thoughts of their own, and feelings, and hopes

The Mysticism of Ordinary and Extraordinary Experience

and dreams. God is in each person as God is in me, and collectively, we are the very heart and soul of God.

And there are some, like Father DiGeorgio, or Mahatma Gandhi, or Yesuahuyh bar Yusef, and many others, whose presence alone reminds one that God is still with us.

In the course of my travels through life, I must have looked into the faces of tens of thousands of people—a distraught woman on a New York subway, a shopkeeper in the old city of Jerusalem begging me to buy something, a child playing alone on a back street in Rome, a childhood friend released from jail for shoplifting to feed his dying mother, anonymous faces in a crowd at a football game. I could not look into the mind of each person and know their joys and sorrows, the pleasure and pain they were experiencing. In the same way, I could not know how and if the same Creator who made their lives possible was sharing in all the infinite details of their collective lives. Can one really look into the soul of God? Does God have a soul? Can a person really know God?

When God spoke to the psalmist and told him to "be still and know that I am God" (Ps 46:10), how much comprehension was God expecting? Theology is the study of God, as if God can be known through knowledge. The meaning of this directive from the psalmist is to relax and stop striving or struggling and simply be aware of the presence of God. We know by not knowing, by not using words—adjectives and descriptive phrases—to define (and limit) God.

The fourteenth century was a turbulent time with wars raging across Europe. The Hundred Years War between England and France and their allies engulfed much of the continent in the continuous fighting over the dynastic ambitions of the houses of Plantagenet and Valois. The Black Death of 1347–1351 resulted in the loss of one-third to one-half of the European population. This caused people to rethink their religious faith. Many laid the rat at the door of the Jews as widespread purges and pogroms were inflicted upon them. Most, however, saw the plague as a sign of God's wrath punishing them for their sins and lack of faith. There was a great desire to know God and God's will for humanity.

The institutional church in Rome was of no help. In fact, the church was often part of the problem. Seeds of Reformation were being sown and many religious thinkers disseminated their thoughts to a populace looking for answers. Among them were the mystics such as Richard Rolle, Catherine of Sienna, Julian of Norwich, the Rhineland mystic, Meister Eckhart,

Entering the Cloud of Unknowing

and his students Johannes Tauler and Henry Suso. From their monastic cells they all advocated a contemplative life of going within and knowing the love of God directly.

Sometime in the latter part of the fourteenth century an unknown English mystic wrote a short book called *The Cloud of Unknowing and the Book of Privy Counseling*. His views were no doubt influenced by Neo-Platonism and Pseudo-Dionysus the Areopagite. He said that we cannot know God and shouldn't bother trying. It is enough just to love God. Our human senses and intellect just get in the way.

I think the author of the *Cloud* had some affinity with Buddhism, particularly Zen, which told its adherents not to think so much on God, but simply be in God's presence and be aware of God's presence in one's own life and in the lives of others.

Our lives are often shaped by the people we know. Father DiGeorgio helped me see the Christ in the love expressed by others.

Make Light of Yourself

I HAVE A FASCINATION for the quality of light. Perhaps it was because light has always been a symbol for the presence of God and the awareness of who we really are. According to Genesis, the electromagnetic spectrum was the first act of creation when God said, "Let there be light." Imagine, four thousand years before Einstein, the ancient Hebrews saw the relativity of light and energy. Genesis begins with an explosion of light. We began in light.

Later, God would appear to Moses in fire, and the symbol of God's presence in the Temple would be the *Ner Tamid*, the eternal lamp. The lighting of the lamps on Hanukkah would represent God's continuing presence. It was commonly believed that when we pass over to the next life, our spiritual form will be that of light and will be attracted to the greater light of God and that of all spiritual beings. This belief is consistent with the literature of the near-death experience where a so-called "being of light" is encountered who provides guidance and instruction.

Apparently, God as light is a universal archetype. The chief god of the ancient Greeks was Zeus, a sky-god, known through lightning and thunder. When Akhenaten introduced a short-lived Egyptian monotheism, the god he worshiped was Amun-Ra, the sun-god. El was the Canaanite god of light and power whose name was brought into the Hebrew culture, given a plural ending, Elohim, and used as another name for Yahweh. The magi who followed the star to Bethlehem were most likely Zoroastrian priests and devotees of Ahura Mazda, the Persian god of light. (You may remember the Mazda Corporation that manufactured light bulbs. Now it's the name of a small car which I suppose we are to fantasize travels at the speed of light.) Lucifer, whom we equate with the devil, was a fallen angel whose name

Make Light of Yourself

means "bearer of light." Virtually all of earth's religions, both ancient and modern, worshiped light in one form or another.

Perhaps, because in a very real sense, we ourselves are light. The substance of our bodies is the product of light. Whether we are animal-eaters or vegetarians, the food we eat derives from plants produced by photosynthesis—from light. We need light to survive.

There are those who suffer from seasonal affective disorders (SAD). When we are deprived of light, we enter into a winter depression with symptoms of diminished energy, increased sleep, weight gain, social withdrawal, lack of concentration, mood changes, and anxiety. Light is so critical to our physiological and psychological health that it is no wonder the ancient peoples worshiped God as pure light.

When Moses asked to see God, God told him it would be too much for him to bear. If it could be compared to anything, it would be like looking into the explosion of a nuclear bomb or the light from a million suns. *The Tibetan Book of the Dead* says that when you die, you encounter a dazzling light that is so bright that only the spiritually prepared can withstand it. It is only by ridding ourselves of the things of earth, by putting off our mortality that we can be at home in the spiritual realm. This is what the mystics called the *via negativa,* the emptying process, the winnowing and pruning by which we learn to let go and surrender to the light, to a love-force greater than we are. Matthew Fox says in his book, *The Physics of Angels,* that without this emptying, this *kenosis,* we can survive only in such a world as the one we are in.

Janusz Slawinski, writing in *The Journal of Near Death Studies,* said, "All living organisms emit low-intensity light; at the time of death, that radiation is ten to 1,000 times stronger than that emitted under normal conditions. This "death flash" is independent of the cause of death, and reflects in intensity and duration the rate of dying . . . The electromagnetic field produced by necrotic radiation, containing energy, internal structure, and information, may permit continuation of consciousness beyond the death of the body."[1]

There are healing modalities, such as *jyorei,* that use the transmission of light to affect healing and induce harmony, and we know the many benefits of light therapy. We are indeed beings of light, emanating from the One Light. Therefore, if we would fly like the angels, we must make light of ourselves.

---

1. "Electromagnetic Radiation and the Afterlife," 79.

To See Ourselves

When I was a child of five or six, I would go to the immense sandbox at a city park and create my imaginary world. One day I saw a man in his twenties standing on the other side of the sandbox. He looked at me, somewhat puzzled, but with a degree of familiarity. I seemed to know him, and he seemed to know me. I asked him, "Who are you?"

He said, "I am you." Oh, no! Some college kid trying to play with my mind. "I am what you could be. I was who you are," he said.

"I am who you may be." Are there parallel universes where we live different lives and every so often, whether in a dream or flash of recognition, we catch a glimpse of another self, or an aspect of ourselves?

But stranger yet, some twenty years after the sandbox visitation, I had a dream in which I visited my past and saw a child playing in a sandbox. He stared at me and asked, "Who are you?" And I said, "I am you."

It is said that when a person sees his *doppelganger*, his spiritual double, it is a sign of an imminent exit from this life. However, sometimes it is a dimensional shift or a wrinkle in time.

The German poet, Johann Wolfgang von Goethe, was riding on the road to Drusenheim in the eighteenth century when he saw his double riding toward him. His doppelganger was wearing a gray suit with gold trim. Eight years later, Goethe was again traveling on the same road, but in the opposite direction. He then realized he was wearing the very gray suit trimmed in gold that he had seen on his double eight years earlier! Had I been Goethe on that first encounter I think I might have stopped for a brief conversation.

Emily Sagée was a French schoolteacher who taught in Wolmar in present-day Latvia. During one particular class session, while Sagée was writing on the blackboard, her exact double appeared next to her, mimicking her every move. When she wrote on the blackboard, the spiritual double also wrote, but without the chalk. The event was witnessed by thirteen of her students. This was only one of several manifestations witnessed by groups of people, not always with the parallel gestures. Although Sagée said that she never saw her doppelganger, her students said that Sagée appeared pale and listless whenever her double appeared, as though it was draining energy from her.

Many other persons of historical note are said to have seen their doppelgangers. Guy de Maupassant, the French novelist, benefitted from his double who dictated to him, a kind of "ghost writer." He wrote about this experience in his short story "Lui."

The great British poet, Percy Bysshe Shelley, encountered his doppelganger in Italy, who pointed toward the Mediterranean Sea where Shelly was to die shortly thereafter in a boating accident. Both Queen Elizabeth I of England and Abraham Lincoln had waking visions or dreams of themselves as dead some days before their actual deaths.

Doppelgangers differ from cases of bilocation in which a person simultaneously appears in two different locations. The twentieth century Capuchin mystic, Padre Pio, was said to have appeared to groups and individuals at the same time, even though many miles separated them. And Sathya Sai Baba's devotees claimed that he appeared to them, sometimes in the guise of different people. Carlos Castaneda also wrote of bilocation, although his flights of fantasy may have been fueled by mescaline.

The veracity of these experiences, including my own, should not be dependent upon the singular observation of the percipient. However, the fact that history and folklore are replete with so many stories requires continued investigation into these phenomena and their meaning. Are they psychological aberrations, distortions of the space-time continuum, intrusions into the collective unconscious, or a continued mystery of the undiscovered country beyond our present reality?

Lost in the Stars

ALAN PATON'S MAGNIFICENT NOVEL, *Cry, The Beloved Country*, was presented as a musical play, *Lost in the Stars*, written by Maxwell Anderson with music by Kurt Weill. There was a scene at the end of the first act where Stephen Kumalo, a black minister in South Africa learns that his son, Absalom, has killed a white man. He is terrified as he looks out over the city of Johannesburg and a sense of great darkness and alienation comes over him. In his imagination, he reflects back to the beginning of time and sees God holding the stars in the palm of his hand. One small star slips from the Creator's hand and drifts away. It is the planet Earth. God searches for it and promises to take special care that it should never be lost again. Then Kumalo sings these words in "Lost in the Stars":

> I've been walking through the night and the day . . .
> And sometimes it seems maybe God's gone away,
> Forgetting the promise that we heard him say
> And we're lost out here in the stars
> Little stars, big stars
> Blowing through the night,
> And we're lost out here in the stars.

The terror of being alone in the universe and the hunger of our heart for God or for someone or something to explain the reason for what happens to us, is as old as human memory. This yearning echoes through the Old Testament prophets in the cries of the people who know that without God we are lost. "O that you would tear open the heavens and come down, so that the mountains would quake at your presence—as when fire kindles brushwood . . . From ages past no one has heard, no ear has perceived, no eye has seen any God besides you. But you were angry, and we sinned; because you hid yourself we transgressed . . . We all fade like a leaf, and our iniquities, like the wind, take us away. There is no one who calls on your name, or attempts to take hold of you; for you have hidden your face from us (Isa 64:1–7).

In our current *annus horribilis* of 2020, more than ever we have the fear that we are lost without a star or a God to guide us.

Thomas Wolfe, in his preface to *Look, Homeward Angel*, also depicts this sense of "lostness."

> Naked and alone we came into exile. In her dark womb we did not know our mother's face; from the prison of her flesh have we come into the unspeakable and incommunicable prison of this earth . . . O waste of loss, in the hot mazes, lost, among bright stars on this most weary unbright cinder, lost! Remembering speechlessly we seek the great forgotten language, the lost land-end into heaven a stone, a leaf, an unfound door. Where? When?[1]

Are we alone out here in our tiny corner of the universe, forgotten by our Creator as we deal with a seemingly unending list of troubles: racial violence and deaths, social protests, Covid-19, wildfires, hurricanes, gun violence and murders, and an unresponsive, ineffective, and often complicit government? One can almost understand why attendance in mainline churches has significantly diminished.

We have reached beyond the stars and within the atom and have returned in our dismay at the lack of meaning and the absence of answers for the living of our lives. As ancient as Isaiah or as modern as space exploration, the human creature learns through desperately painful lessons that he cannot manufacture a Savior. We need God!

That gnawing emptiness in our lives is a yearning for God. It will not be satisfied by those who offer easy answers to hard questions. The multimillionaire television preachers cannot satisfy spiritual hunger. Materialism cannot quench the thirst for what we so desperately seek. Big Daddy, in Tennessee Williams' play, *Cat On a Hot Tin Roof*, voices the greed and the futility which are marks of our society.

> Yes, sir, boy—the human animal is a beast that dies and if he's got money he buys and buys and buys and I think the reason he buys everything he can buy is that in the back of his mind he has the crazy hope that one of his purchases will be everlasting!—which it never can be. (Act 2)

---

1. Wolfe, *Look Homeward, Angel*, 1.

The Mysticism of Ordinary and Extraordinary Experience

The scriptures remind us over and over again that you cannot be found until you realize that you are lost. The prodigal son does not return to the father until he recognizes he is in the far country. We must have a new perspective on the presence of God in our lives.

A recent CBS 60 Minutes documentary featured the hiring of autistic persons to work in astrophysics to sift through space telescope photos of distant galaxies to find new planets and other meaningful patterns. Many autistic persons are able to process information differently and see things that most people do not. The ability to see beyond seeing could help all of us realize that we are not lost among the stars. We are all different like an infinite array of stars, but we are all part of one universe, all part of God. Our salvation is in the realization that we are all in process, that God is greater than our comprehension, and that we are moving toward the infinite expression of universal love. That hope is expressed in Stephen Kumalo's conclusion in "Lost in the Stars":

> Now a man don't mind if the stars grow dim
> And the clouds blow over and darken him,
> So long as the Lord God's watching over them,
> Keeping track how it all goes on.

Killing the Buddha

IN VISITING THE CHURCHES and cathedrals of Italy a few years ago, I saw so many images captured by the great artists on the walls of these places of worship. Michelangelo, Donizetti, Giotto, Cimabue, Leonardo all tried to capture the glory and majesty of their faith so that other Christians could catch a glimpse of God, the God who was revealed through the incarnation in Jesus of Nazareth. But it was only a reflection. It was their interpretation rendered in paint. I was viewing their work some five hundred years later from a different cultural context and theological background and interpreting altogether differently than perhaps the artists intended. What I was seeing was only a reflection of light.

In a church in Edinburgh that I had visited in my student days, there was a beehive of activity. They had a family shelter. Children were being cared for. Street people were coming in to get meals. The bulletin board indicated a ministry to those addicted to alcohol and drugs. And later in my Celtic journey I entered an ancient church on the isle of Iona where a group of Christians prayed for the peace of the world, for environmental healing, and for the reconciliation of nations. These two churches represented a different reflection of the gospel in the search for social justice. One could see the face of God in those who were working and struggling for peace in the world.

A traveling art exhibition at one of our local university galleries depicted how various artists see and interpret God. The mixed media show sought to represent how God was understood by these creative minds. One gets the impression that we see God through the lenses of our own needs, desires, experiences and interests. God was portrayed as Love and as Hate, as a Creator and Destroyer, as One who heals and as One who suffers with us. While some of the artists demonstrated how various parts of our culture

The Mysticism of Ordinary and Extraordinary Experience

understood God, for the most part the artist went within and represented the meaning of God in the artist's own life. God always finds expression within the person.

When I was in college, I would occasionally attend Quaker meetings at an old meeting house in Phoenixville, Pennsylvania. It was a one-room house with a bit of a vestibule and nothing more than hard benches and a solitary table. In the quiet calm and silence of that meeting house, I saw another face of God, the God that dwelled in the inner light of my own soul, but was also reflected in the light that broke forth from those around me as we shared our inspired thoughts and looked for a sense of meeting, a common discernment of the collective voice of God.

I once sat at table with a group from Georgia. In spite of the language barrier, one man, a retired minister, was telling me of a church near Atlanta that has some 30,000 members, so large that the parking lot has shuttle trams like Disney World. He asked rhetorically how the senior minister at that church could minister to anyone other than his own staff. One must sacrifice intimacy for the sake of the security and the assurance of numbers. The larger the community, the less community there is. It is yet another reflection of how people come face to face with God.

Where do you come face to face with your God? You may go from church to church on your spiritual quest. You may try different forms of worship. You may gather with people of many backgrounds and traditions. You may seek your own private relationship with God through personal prayer and meditation. Where is God to be found?

In words often attributed to Teresa of Avila, she once said, "Whose hands but our hands are God's hands?" Well, whose faces but our faces are God's face? How do we reflect God to one another? When we sit face to face, look into one another's eyes, when we see another and they know it, and feel listened to, affirmed, somehow more real, aren't we for a moment the face of the divine for them? Gandhi once said that to the hungry man God appears in the form of bread. God is what people are desperately looking for; God is whatever they feel is their deepest need. And the deepest need for all of us is to feel that we are loved and that we are connected, that we truly belong.

The Pharisees asked Jesus, "What is the greatest commandment?" Jesus replied with the answer that would satisfy their greatest need: "You shall love the Lord your God with all your heart, and with all your soul, and with all your mind" (Luke 10:27). And the way that you demonstrate or show your love for God is to "love your neighbor as yourself" (Luke 10:27).

Killing the Buddha

The mystics of the church sought to do precisely that, to achieve union with God by being what God is: pure love; to merge their soul with the heart of God; to be of one mind with the will of God. You can spend your entire life looking for God, but as God said to Jeremiah, "When you seek me, you will find me; if you seek me with all your heart" (Jer 29:13).

You cannot go to a place to meet God face to face. You carry God within you, and you must discover that yourself, and realize that the God in you needs to connect to the divine that is in every other person. It is only in relationship that we realize the God within us.

A Zen Master once warned a disciple, "If you meet the Buddha on the road, kill him."[1] It was his way of saying that no meaning that comes from outside of us is real. God is within us. Killing the Buddha outside is destroying the false idols that lure us from realizing that we are created to love one another and to be at peace with the world.

I once officiated at a wedding of a Muslim woman whose parents had come from Kosova and a Southern Baptist man from Georgia. The couple had requested that in order to honor both traditions, no specific references should be made to either the Islamic faith or the Christian faith, though I could use the sacred writings of both. What I found to be most important in both faith traditions were relations with each other and with God. How we relate to one another is how we relate to God, and that is what we celebrated.

The Creator of the universe is not going to be concerned about to what denomination we belong or whether we worship in a church, mosque, ashram, or synagogue, but how we are able to love one another and recognize and meld with that divine love that is in each person. When we come face to face with God at the last judgment, according to Jesus, we will not be judged on the basis of our intellect, or our ability to recite a creed, or how many of the enemy we can kill for Jesus or Allah, or what version of the Lord's Prayer we use in our worship. We will be judged solely on the basis of how we are able to love and how we are able to reflect that love in our relationship with others: "for I was hungry and you gave me food, I was thirsty and you gave me something to drink, I was a stranger and you welcomed me, I was naked and you gave me clothing, I was sick and you took care of me, I was in prison and you visited me" (Matt 25:34).

Let us strive with all our heart, soul, and mind to be one with God who is love. Let us come face to face with that God and to realize what God's intention is for us.

1. Kopp, *If You Meet the Buddha on the Road, Kill Him*, 188.

Bibliography

Alegretti, Wagner. *Retrocognitions: An Investigation into Memories of Past Lives and the Period Between Lives*. Miami: International Academy of Consciousness. 2004.
Antelme, Ruth Schumann, and Stéphane Rossini. *Becoming Osiris*. Rochester: Inner Traditions, 1998.
Archiati, Pietro. *Reincarnation in Modern Life: Toward a New Christian Awareness*. London: Temple Lodge, 1997.
Bache, Christopher M. *Lifecycles, Reincarnation and the Web of Life*. St. Paul: Paragon House, 1991.
Badham, Paul, and Linda Badham. *Death and Immortality in the Religions of the World*. St. Paul: Paragon House, 1987.
Baker, Mark C., and Stewart Goetz. *The Soul Hypothesis*. New York: Continuum, 2011.
Berendt, Joachim-Ernst. *The World Is Sound: Nada Brahma, Music and the Landscape of Consciousness*. Rochester: Destiny, 1983.
Berliner, Paul F. *Thinking in Jazz: The Infinite Art of Improvisation*. Chicago: University of Chicago Press, 1994.
Bowman, Carol. *Children's Past Lives*. New York: Bantam, 1998.
———. *Return from Heaven*. New York: Harper Torch, 2003.
Bradley, Ian. *The Celtic Way*. London: Longman and Todd, 1993.
Brother Lawrence of the Resurrection [Nicholas Herman]. *The Practice of the Presence of God*. Translated by Salvatore Sciurba. Washington, DC: ICS, 1994.
Bucke, Richard Maurice. *Cosmic Consciousness: A Study in the Evolution of the Human Mind*. Secaucus: Citadel, 1961.
Butcher, Carmen Acevedo. *St. Hildegard of Bingen—Doctor of the Church*. Brewster: Paraclete, 2007.
Cahill, Thomas. *How the Irish Saved Civilization*. New York: Doubleday, 1995.
Campbell, Don. *The Mozart Effect: Tapping the Power of Music to Heal the Body, Strengthen the Mind, and Unlock the Creative Spirit*. New York: Avon, 1997.
Catherine of Siena. *The Dialogue*. Classics of Western Spirituality. New York: Paulist, 1980.
Cerminara, Gina. *Many Mansions: The Edgar Cayce Story on Reincarnation*. New York: Signet, 1988.
Chadwick, Nora K. *The Celts*. London: Pelican, 1970.
———. *The Druids*. Cardiff: University of Wales Press, 1966.
Church, Dawson. *Mind to Matter*. Carlsbad: Hay House, 2018.
Cranston, Sylvia, and Carey Williams. *Reincarnation: A New Horizon in Science, Religion, and Society*. Pasadena: Theosophical University Press, 1993.

Bibliography

Crow, Bill. *Jazz Anecdotes*. New York: Oxford University Press, 1990.
Csikszentmihalyi, Mihaly. *Flow: The Psychology of Optimal Experience*. New York: Harper, 1990.
Cumont, Franz. *After Life in Roman Paganism*. New York: Yale University Press, 1922.
Cunliffe, Barry. *The Ancient Celts*. London: Oxford University Press, 1997.
Danelek, J. Allan. *The Case for Reincarnation: Unraveling the Mysteries of the Soul*. St. Paul: Llewellyn, 2010.
Doherty, Catherine de Hueck. *Poustinia: Christian Spirituality of the East for Western Man*. Notre Dame: Ave Maria, 1974.
Duthie, Charles S. *Resurrection and Immortality*. London: Bagster & Sons, 1979.
Ellis, Peter Berresford. *The Druids*. Grand Rapids: Eerdmans, 1994.
Evans-Wentz, W. Y. *The Tibetan Book of the Dead*. New York: Oxford University Press, 1960.
Eylon, Dina Ripsman. *Reincarnation in Jewish Mysticism and Gnosticism*. Lewiston: Edwin Mellen, 2003.
Finucane, Ronald C. *Ghosts: Appearances of the Dead and Cultural Transformation*. Amherst: Prometheus, 1996.
Fox, Matthew. *The Coming of the Cosmic Christ*. San Francisco: Harper & Row, 1988.
———. *Original Blessing*. Santa Fe: Bear & Co., 1983.
———, and Rupert Sheldrake. *The Physics of Angels: Exploring the Realm Where Science and Spirit Meet*. San Francisco: Harper, 1996.
Fyfe, James. *The Hereafter*. Edinburgh: T&T Clark, 1890.
Gaster, T. H. "The Abode of the Dead." In *The Interpreter's Dictionary of the Bible*, vol. A–D, 787–88. Nashville: Abingdon, 1962.
Gennep, Arnold van. *The Rites of Passage*. 2nd ed. Chicago: University of Chicago Press, 2019.
Gilchrist, Alexander. *The Life of William Blake*. Edited by W. Graham Robertson. Mineola: Dover, 2017.
Glass, Bentley. "Cell and Psyche: The Biology of Purpose by Edmund W. Sinnott." *The Quarterly Review of Biology* 27.1 (1952) 62.
Goldhill, Olivia. "The Idea that Everything from Spoons to Stones Is Conscious Is Gaining Academic Credibility." *Quartz* (January 27, 2018). https://qz.com/1184574/the-idea-that-everything-from-spoons-to-stones-are-conscious-is-gaining-academic-credibility/.
Gowan, John Curtis. *Trance, Art and Creativity*. Buffalo: Creative Education Foundation, 1975.
Guirdham, Arthur. *The Cathars & Reincarnation*. New York: C. W. Daniel Co., 2004.
Harkness, Georgia. *Mysticism: It's Meaning and Message*. Nashville: Abingdon, 1973.
Head, Joseph, and S. L. Cranston, eds. *Reincarnation: The Phoenix Fire Mystery*. New York: Julian, 1994.
Hohman, John George. *Pow-Wows, or Long Lost Friend: A Collection of Mysterious and Invaluable Arts and Remedies, for Man as Well as Animals*. Brooklyn: FultonReligious Supply, 1820.
Howe, J. Quincy. *Reincarnation for the Christian*, Pasadena: Theosophical, 1987.
Jacob, Edmond. *Theology of the Old Testament*. New York: Harper, 1958.
James, William. *The Varieties of Religious Experience*. New York: The New American Library of World Literature, 1958.

Bibliography

Jefferson, Warren. "Reincarnation Beliefs of North American Indians: Soul Journeys, Metamorphoses, and Near-Death Experiences." Summertown: Native Voices, 2009.

Johnston, William, ed. *The Cloud of Unknowing and The Book of Privy Counseling.* Garden City: Image, 1973.

Josephus, Flavius. *The War of the Jews.* Translated by William Whiston. Overland: Digireads, 2020.

Joyce, Timothy. *Celtic Christianity.* Maryknoll: Orbis, 1998.

Katz, Steven T. "The Conservative Character of Mystical Experience." In *Mysticism and Religious Traditions*, 3–60. New York: Oxford University Press, 1983.

Kopp, Sheldon B. *If You Meet the Buddha on the Road, Kill Him: The Pilgrimage of Psychotherapy Patients.* New York: Bantam, 1972.

Leininger, Bruce, and Andrea Leininger. *Soul Survivor: The Reincarnation of a World War II Fighter Pilot.* New York: Grand Central, 2009.

Leland, Kurt. *Otherwhere: A Field Guide to Nonphysical Reality for the Out-of-Body Traveler.* Charlottesville: Hampton Roads, 2001.

———. *The Unanswered Question: Death, Near-Death, and the Afterlife.* Charlottesville: Hampton Roads, 2002.

Leonard, Neil. *Jazz-Myth and Religion.* New York: Oxford University Press, 1987.

Llewelyn, Robert. *All Shall Be Well: The Spirituality of Julian of Norwich for Today.* New York: Paulist, 1982.

Lommel, Pim van. *Consciousness Beyond Life: The Science of the Near-Death Experience.* New York: HarperCollins, 2010.

Lonnerstrand, Sture. *I Have Lived Before: The True Story of the Reincarnation of Shanti Devi.* Huntsville: Ozark Mountain, 1998.

Louth, Andrew. *The Origins of the Christian Mystical Tradition: From Plato to Denys.* Oxford: Clarendon, 1981.

MacGregor, Geddes. *Reincarnation in Christianity.* Wheaton: Quest, 1978.

McEneaney, Bonnie. *Messages: Signs, Visits and Premonitions from Loved Ones Lost on 9/11.* New York: HarperCollins, 2010.

McDannell, Colleen, and Bernhard Lang. *Heaven: A History.* New York: Vintage, 1990.

Matthew, Caitlin. *The Celtic Spirit: Daily Meditations for the Turning Year.* San Francisco: Harper, 1998.

Matthews, Caitlin, and John Matthews. *The Encyclopedia of Celtic Wisdom.* Rockport: Element, 1994.

Martino, Pat. *Here and Now: The Autobiography of Pat Martino.* Milwaukee: Backbeat, 2011.

Miller, Sukie. *After Death.* New York: Touchstone, 1997.

Mills, Robert. *Suspended Animation: Pain, Pleasure and Punishment in Medieval Culture.* London: Reaktion, 2012.

Monroe, Robert A. *Journeys Out of the Body.* New York: Doubleday, 1971.

Moody, Raymond A., Jr. *Life After Life.* Covington: Mockingbird, 1975.

Newell, J. Philip. *One Foot in Eden: A Celtic View of the Stages of Life.* Mahwah: Paulist Press, 1999.

Oderberg, I. M. "Reincarnation as Taught by Early Christians." https://www.theosophy-nw.org/theosnw/reincar/re-imo.htm.

O'Donohue, John. *Anam Cara.* New York: HarperCollins, 1997.

O'Laughlin, Thomas. *Journeys On the Edge: The Celtic Tradition.* Maryknoll: Orbis, 2000.

Osis, Karlis, and Erlendur Haralsson. *At the Hour of Death.* New York: Avon, 1977.

Bibliography

Otto, Rudolf. *The Idea of the Holy*. 2nd ed. Translated by John W. Harvey. New York: Oxford University Press, 1958.

Pemberton, Cinta. *Soulfaring: Celtic Pilgrimage Then and Now*. London: SPCK, 1999.

Penner, Hans H. "The Mystical Illusion." In *Mysticism and Religious Traditions*, edited by Steven T. Katz, 89–116. Oxford: Oxford University Press, 1983.

Pennick, Nigel. *Celtic Sacred Landscapes*. New York: Thames and Hudson, 1996.

Pew Research Center. "'New Age' beliefs common among both religious and nonreligious Americans." https://www.pewresearch.org/fact-tank/2018/10/01/new-age-beliefs-common-among-both-religious-and-nonreligious-americans/.

———. *The Sacred World of the Celts*. Rochester: Inner Traditions International, 1997.

Porter, Lewis. *John Coltrane: His Life and Music*. Ann Arbor: University of Michigan Press, 2000.

Prophet, Elizabeth Clare, and Erin L. Prophet. *Reincarnation: The Missing Link in Christianity*. Corwin Springs: Summit University Press, 1997.

Rabey, Steve. *In the House of Memory: Ancient Celtic Wisdom for Everyday Life*. New York: Penguin Putnam, 1998.

Ring, Kenneth. *Life at Death: A Scientific Investigation of the Near-Death Experience*. New York: William Morrow & Co., 1982.

Rogo, D. Scott. *The Search for Yesterday: A Critical Examination of the Evidence for Reincarnation*. Upper Saddle River: Prentice-Hall, 1985.

Sagan, Carl. *Broca's Brain: Reflections on the Romance of Science*. New York: Random House, 1974.

———. *Demon Haunted World*. New York: Random House. 1996.

Sellner, Edward. "Celtic Spirituality and Prayer." *Praying* 74 (September–October 1996) 4–9.

Selzer, Adam. *Ghosts of Lincoln*. Woodbury: Llewellyn Worldwide, 2015.

Serio, Harry L. *The Dwelling Place of Wonder*. Eugene: Wipf and Stock, 2016.

Shroder, Tom. *Old Souls: The Scientific Evidence for Past Lives*. New York: Simon & Schuster, 1999.

Silf, Margaret. *Sacred Spaces: Stations on a Celtic Way*. Brewster: Paraclete, 2001.

Sinnott, Edmund W. *The Biology of the Spirit*. Los Angeles: Science of Mind Publications, 1955.

Slawinski, Janusz. "Electromagnetic Radiation and the Afterlife." *Journal of Near-Death Studies* 6 (1987) 79–94. https://doi.org/10.1007/BF01073390.

Smith, Margaret. *The Way of the Mystics: The Early Christian Mystics and the Rise of the Sufis*. New York: Oxford University Press, 1978.

Stace, W. T. *Mysticism and Philosophy*. Los Angeles: Jeremy P. Tarcher, 1986.

Steiner, Rudolf. *Reincarnation and Immortality*. New York: Harper Collins, 1980.

———. *Reincarnation and Karma: Two Fundamental Truths of Existence*. Hudson: Steiner, 1992.

———. *A Western Approach to Reincarnation and Karma: Selected Lectures and Writings*. Edited and Introduced by Rene Querido. Hudson: Anthroposophic Press, 1997.

Stevenson, Ian. *Children Who Remember Previous Lives: A Question of Reincarnation*. Revised ed. Jefferson: McFarland & Company, 2000.

———. *Reincarnation and Biology: A Contribution to the Etiology of Birthmarks and Birth Defects*. Westport: Praeger, 1997.

———. *Twenty Cases Suggestive of Reincarnation*. 2nd ed. Charlottesville: University of Virginia Press, 1980.

Bibliography

Szarmach, Paul E., ed. *An Introduction to the Medieval Mystics of Europe*. Albany: State University of New York Press, 1984.

Tart, Charles. *The End of Materialism: How Evidence of the Paranormal Is Bringing Science and Spirit Together*. Oakland: New Harbinger, 2009.

Tucker, Jim B. *Life Before Life: A Scientific Investigation of Children's Memories of Past Lives*. New York: St. Martin's, 2005.

Turner, Victor. *The Ritual Process: Structure and Anti-Structure*. London: Routledge, 1995.

Underhill, Evelyn. *Mysticism: A Study in the Nature and Development of Man's Spiritual Consciousness*, 12th edition. New York: Dutton, 1961.

———. *The Mystics of the Church*. New York: Schoken, 1964.

Wambach, Helen. *Life Before Life*. New York: Bantam, 1979.

Weiss, Brian L. *Many Lives, Many Masters*. New York: Fireside, 1988.

Wentz, Richard E., ed. *Pennsylvania Dutch Folk Spirituality*. New York: Paulist, 1993.

Wilber, Ken. *The Holographic Paradigm and Other Paradoxes*. Boston: Shambhala, 1991.

———. *The Spectrum of Consciousness*. Pasadena: First Quest, 1977.

Wolfe, Thomas. *Look Homeward, Angel*. New York: Charles Scribner's Sons, 1929.

Yeats, W. B. *The Celtic Twilight: Myth, Fantasy and Folklore*. Bridport: Prism, 1893.

www.ingramcontent.com/pod-product-compliance
Lightning Source LLC
Chambersburg PA
CBHW051926160426
43198CB00012B/2054